A YOUNG ADULT'S GUIDE
TO PERSONAL FINANCE

A Young Adult's Guide to
PERSONAL
FINANCE

It's Time to Move Out of Your Parents' Basement
MIKE McGUINNESS

www.mascotbooks.com

For more information, please contact:
Mascot Books
620 Herndon Parkway #320
Herndon, VA 20170
info@mascotbooks.com

Library of Congress Control Number: 2018903295

CPSIA Code: PRBVG0518A
ISBN-13: 978-1-64307-026-1

Printed in the United States

TO MY WIFE MARY, or Saint Mary as she is known to my family—and at least one of my former students. She has always supported me in whatever I have ventured into. I am always amazed by the uncanny knack she has of bringing out the best in kids and making them feel at ease.

She was the original special education teacher of the year in New Hampshire and, to this day, we will still run into former students who enthusiastically greet her and talk about events that occurred many years ago as if they were yesterday. She was an original board member of Friends in Action in Portsmouth, New Hampshire, an organization that puts together social events for individuals with developmental disabilities. It was always a pleasure to watch friendships flourish through the work of this organization.

She did a great job raising our kids when I was frequently on the road and juggled our family life with her work in special education. I now marvel at what she accomplishes as she enjoys her role as a grandmother.

Thanks for all your love and support over the years.

CONTENTS

THE POWER OF COMPOUND INTEREST

STUDENT: I have heard that Albert Einstein called compound interest the "Eighth Wonder of the World." Can you explain compound interest to me and what it can do for me?

PROFESSOR: He actually said, "The power of compounding is the eighth wonder of the world. One who understands it, earns it, and the one who does not pays it." (Anand, 2016)

S: Can you explain compound interest to me?

P: Easily done, with simple interest, interest is paid on the original investment. Thus, if you invested $100 at 6 percent, you would earn $6 in the first year and $6 in the second year giving you $112 at the end of two years. With compound interest, you earn interest on interest. Thus the $100 invested for two years would give you $112.36 at the end of two years. You have earned an extra 36 cents of interest on the $6 of interest from the first year.

S: Wow, an extra 36 cents, I can't even get a candy bar with that.

P: No you can't, but those numbers merely illustrate the concept. How much do you want to make when you leave the college?

S: I want to make $50,000 minimum when I leave.

P: Pretty good and I have to strongly advise that you save at least $3,000, so I will use that number to illustrate. Let's say you borrow $3,000 from your parents. They have made the loan with the proviso that you invest it and you only need to repay them the $3,000 after 10 years. We'll use simple interest first. Thus, you put away $3,000 right now and let's optimistically say you earn 4 percent per year for 10 years, so at the end of 10 years, you will have $4,200.

S: Not bad on my part. I increased my money by 40 percent and I don't know anything about investing.

P: Clearly. If you had invested it with compound interest over 10 years, you would now have $4,440 or 5.7 percent more.

S: I am still not impressed by this at all.

P: Well, we have just used one lump sum and I am hoping you are investing each year. But just to stay with the previous example of the $3,000 for now, what if you could earn 8 percent per year? With simple interest, you would have $5,400 at the end of 10 years.

S: Big deal, so using your logic, 5.7 percent more would make it $5,708, or $308 more. I still can't get excited about that.

P: I understand your thought process, but you are a bit off. At 8 percent per year compounded, your $3,000 would be worth $6,477, or almost 20 percent more. At higher rates, the compounding factor becomes worth more.

S: Wow! That is a big difference. Where are you getting all these numbers from?

P: I'll give you a small table here (Table 1) which shows the future value of a dollar. Just select a dollar amount, settle on how long you can put it away for, and your assumed interest rate. Using the $3,000 at 8 percent that we just discussed, you will see that the factor for 8 percent and 10 years is 2.159, so $3,000 times 2.159 equals $6,477.

FUTURE VALUE OF A DOLLAR
TABLE 1

	4%	5%	6%	7%	8%
1	1.040	1.050	1.060	1.070	1.080
2	1.082	1.103	1.124	1.145	1.166
3	1.125	1.158	1.191	1.225	1.260
4	1.170	1.216	1.262	1.311	1.360
5	1.217	1.276	1.338	1.403	1.469
6	1.265	1.340	1.419	1.501	1.587
7	1.316	1.407	1.504	1.606	1.714
8	1.369	1.477	1.594	1.718	1.851
9	1.423	1.551	1.689	1.838	1.999
10	1.480	1.629	1.791	1.967	2.159

S: I see, I like this little table.

P: It is even easier. There are many financial websites that will do this for you. The concept is the time value of money and I will use many variations of it during our discussions. Now back to your incentive to save, I hope you are putting away at least 6 percent (and I recommend more) of your gross salary each year to allow you to buy your house, give it away, or whatever your goals and aspirations are. Now that you see the point, imagine what you can put away if you save money each year.

S: I'll bite. What if I save $3,000 per year? I don't borrow from my parents and I save it at the end of each year for the next 10 years. How much will I have if I earn 4 percent? Do you have a magical little table for that?

P: Ignoring you sarcasm, I actually do. Here is a table (Table 2) for the same amount invested at the end of each year. Tell me how much you will have if you invest $3,000 at the end of each of the next 10 years.

	FUTURE VALUE OF A SERIES OF ANNUAL DEPOSITS TABLE 2				
	4%	5%	6%	7%	8%
1	1.000	1.000	1.000	1.000	1.000
2	2.040	2.050	2.060	2.070	2.080
3	3.122	3.153	3.184	3.215	3.246
4	4.246	4.310	4.375	4.440	4.506
5	5.416	5.526	5.637	5.751	5.867
6	6.633	6.802	6.975	7.153	7.336
7	7.898	8.142	8.394	8.654	8.923
8	9.214	9.549	9.897	10.260	10.637
9	10.583	11.027	11.491	11.978	12.488
10	12.006	12.578	13.181	13.816	14.487

S: Well $3,000 times 12.006 gives me $36,018 at the end of 10 years.

P: Nice job with the magical table! Once again, I will give you unsolicited advice. Your salary is increasing each year so you should be saving more each year which only serves to increase your return.

S: This is starting to get interesting. If I could earn 8 percent on the $3,000 I am saving at the end of each of the next 10 years, I will have $43,461 ($3,000 * 14.487). I like this compound interest thing. Any there any downsides?

P: Not from the investing viewpoint, but there certainly is from the spending standpoint. Give me one of your goals.

S: Well, let's say I want to send one of my children to Saint A's in, say, 25 years.

P: Okay, I have calculated that the "all in" cost (tuition, room and board, and mandatory fees) has increased at an annualized rate of 6.84 percent from 1978 to the current school year. Increases have been lower in recent years with low inflation, so let's use an average 4 percent increase for the next 25 years.

S: Oh no! I think I know where this is going.

P: You certainly do. If the current year "all in" cost of Saint A's increases by 4 percent per year for the next 25 years, the total cost will be $144,327 in 25 years.

S: Any other places where compounding is a negative?

P: There certainly are. I'll use auto loans and mortgages as an example. Miss a payment and you have a penalty, and now interest is being calculated on interest so the compounding is a big negative.

S: So you are telling me what you originally portrayed as a big positive is actually a big negative?

P: Not at all, it depends on the individual, and how they manage the money they have. It depends on how you manage your money in many areas, which I hope we can discuss throughout the semester. Remember Einstein's quote with respect to interest.

The key for you is, the earlier you start saving the better off you are going to be.

S: Well, I want to have some fun early so I will start saving when I am 35.

P: Big mistake, my young friend. You must not have heard me when I said the earlier you start, the better off you are going to be.

S: If I save from 35 to 65, I will do just fine.

P: You'll do okay, but let's look at the numbers. I have conjured up another "magical" table (Table 3) for you. We'll keep the numbers simple as it will illustrate the point. Let's say you make $50,000 per year and you save 10 percent of that each year.

S: Well, that's $5,000, and if I save $5,000 at the end of each year for the next 30 years and am earning 4 percent interest, what will that give me?

FUTURE VALUE OF A SERIES OF ANNUAL DEPOSITS
TABLE 3

	4%	5%	6%	7%	8%
10	12.006	12.578	13.181	13.816	14.487
20	29.778	33.066	36.786	40.995	45.762
25	41.646	47.727	54.865	63.249	73.106
30	56.085	66.439	79.058	94.461	113.283
35	73.652	90.320	111.435	138.237	172.317
40	95.026	120.800	154.762	199.635	259.057

P: Well, looking at the table I have given you, what is the factor for 30 years at 4 percent?

S: It looks like 56.085, so $5,000 multiplied by 56.085 gives me $280,425.

P: Well, does saving 10 years earlier make a difference? What about the $5,000 invested at 4 percent for 40 years?

S: The factor there is 95.026 so that would give me $475,130. I hate to admit it, but you appear to be right.

P: Thanks for that small concession. Just for the sake of argument, what if you can earn 8 percent a year for the 30 years and 40 years we looked at?

S: 30 years at 8 percent is 113.283, and 40 years at 8 percent is 259.057. Yikes! We are talking about $566,415 and $1,295,285 ($5,000 * 259.057). Wow!

P: And hopefully you'll be getting raises each year, which only explodes those numbers even more.

When you work, you may be eligible to be in a 401K or 403b plan, whereby your employer matches a percentage of what you save, which only drives those numbers higher. You need to be saving at least the minimum amount, which allows you to receive the maximum match from the employer.

S: Minimum, maximum. I am quite confused.

P: As you may initially be with many of the things we will discuss. We'll go through the specifics of many areas including a review of an employee benefits package. By the end, you will know the basics and be in a position to ask the questions that need to be asked in each area, hopefully.

BUDGETING

STUDENT: Scary to say, I have always hated anything to do with numbers, but I am starting to find this personal finance topic interesting. Do you mind if we discuss various areas at different times?

PROFESSOR: Certainly not. I am glad you are interested because too many people develop an interest well after the point they should have. The end result is that they find themselves in financial difficulties that may have avoided with better decision making.

S: I certainly want to avoid that. What area would be useful for me right now?

P: Without a doubt, that would be budgeting. If you develop good budgeting practices at this time in your life, it will benefit you throughout your lifetime.

S: What exactly is budgeting?

P: In its simplest form, it is knowing how much you have to spend, and prioritizing your spending. If you plan carefully, you can certainly expand your options with respect to spending your money.

S: My parents gave me $1,500 to spend this semester for entertainment, social events, et cetera.

P: Okay, we are in the second week of the semester. How much do you have left?

S: $1,000. My friends and I drove to Montreal this weekend and had a great time. Do you know that you get more Canadian dollars when you exchange U.S. dollars?

P: For sure at this time, but if I follow you correctly, you spent about $500 on this trip?

S: About that, but what a great weekend.

P: You can still have great weekends, but you certainly can't spend like that every weekend. With a 15 week semester, you had approximately $100 each week. With the first week done, you have approximately $71 per week for the rest of the semester.

S: $71 per week?! But I have a few concerts I want to go to and the tickets cost at least that much.

P: Well, you might not be able to make them all. I suggest you budget the rest of the semester carefully to make sure you can do as much as possible, but it definitely looks like you will have budget issues. What are the primary areas where you spend money?

S: Movies, new video games, going out with friends on the weekend.

P: Any idea how much you spend on these in any given month?

S: No, usually my parents will help me out when I am home, but they said college is expensive, money is tight, and I need to live with the $1,500 they have allotted.

P: Well, time for you to prioritize. Take the $1,000 that you have left and divvy it into categories and determine how much you think you will spend in each category.

S: So if I put $50 in the category Movies, that is all I can spend for movies?

P: No, a budget is just a plan. Now you know that if you spend more than $50 for movies, you need to spend less in one or more of your other categories. More importantly for you, I recommend tracking your expenses by category by week for the remainder of the semester. Two of your categories will be Miscellaneous (Other), for items that don't fit neatly into a category, and Don't Remember, which is for money spent for which you cannot account. If you spend more than $10 on something you put in Miscellaneous (Other), make a note of it; you may need another category. If you have too much in Don't Remember, you need to do a better job of tracking your expenses.

You'll be surprised by the financial discipline you will develop that helps you later in life.

S: This gets easier then as you get older?

P: It actually gets harder. Right now, you most likely have just variable expenses.

S: What do you mean by variable expenses?

P: Variable expenses are those that are left to your discretion. You can spend the money or not spend the money and you can vary the amount if necessary. After you graduate and accumulate assets, you will have fixed and variable expenses, and the fixed have to be paid.

S: Give me some examples of fixed expenses.

P: Let's say you own a home. Fixed expenses associated with the home would be: monthly principal and interest; property taxes (and they generally increase every year); and homeowners insurance (which also increases each year). If you have a car loan, that is a fixed expense because your monthly or quarterly car insurance payment is fixed (although you can vary it yearly, which we will discuss later).

Generally, anything that has to be paid and the amount is known each month is a fixed expense. Don't pay it, and the magic of compound interest starts to work against you in addition to any penalties.

Many expenses are semi-variable, which is part fixed and part variable. For instance, your electricity bill has a service component and a consumption component; with your phone plan, it is generally fixed with unlimited calls and data usage, but if you have maximum data usage each month, it is now semi-variable. Even heating oil I would consider semi-variable. While the price per gallon varies, you need to keep the house heated.

Variable expenses are those over which you have the most control. Food is a variable expense to you this semester since you are on the meal plan. Once you leave Saint A's, it is a semi-variable expense. You certainly need to eat, but you can exercise great control over what you are spending for food particularly with respect to going out to eat. Entertainment is a variable expense and weekend entertainment spending is generally a big item for young people. Vacation trips with your friends you can control.

As you get older, you will want to divide your expenses into fixed, semi-variable, or variable categories, and thus you can set your budget accordingly. You want to make sure you can cover all your costs each month. Most importantly is controlling what becomes fixed as those costs are locked in, and then the variable is what you have left to spend from your monthly income.

S: What do you mean by controlling what becomes fixed?

P: The mortgage you take on your home, the price of the car you purchase; in short, the "big ticket" items you may purchase. If you are renting, the monthly rent is a fixed cost so the fancier the rental property, the higher the fixed cost.

S: Can you explain mortgages and buying a car to me?

P: Sure, we'll do that at a later time. For now, let's finish up on budgeting. You will be deducting your fixed costs and projected semi-variable costs from your monthly take home pay, and what you have left can cover variable costs.

S: What do you mean by "take home" pay? I will be taking home everything I have earned, won't I?

P: We'll talk taxes next, but the short answer is no. Now I will discuss the first place that money left over after deducting your fixed and semi-variable expenses should be spent. That is namely on yourself, but in the form of a savings/investment plan. Many financial experts recommend that people save 10 percent of their gross pay every pay period.

S: Wow, after all this, I have no social life as I have nothing left to spend.

P: You should have money left to spend, but spend it wisely. With a proper budgeting plan—I would recommend financial software to help with that—you will be able to plan properly and hopefully work towards achieving your financial goals, which in turn will assist you in reaching your personal goals. Sometimes you may have to bypass good restaurants or a weekend trip away, but the earlier you develop that discipline the better off you will be financially.

S: I understand only as long as I don't have to give up my daily café latte which gets me through the day.

P: I have to recommend finding another way to get through the day. Remember we discussed compound interest. Let's say I can get you to give up your café latte and instead invest the money at the end of the year. Using $3.65 as the cost of your coffee drink, adding a 9 percent sales tax and multiplying by 365 means you would have an extra $1,452 at the end of each year to invest if you give up your daily coffee. If you can invest that amount for 30 years and earn 4 percent interest on it, you will have $81,435 at the end of 30 years.

S: And I have to assume that the price will not be $3.65 for the 30 years so the $81,435 will be far higher?

P: You are learning quickly!

TAXES FOR THE NEW GRADUATE

STUDENT: Everyone tells me I will have to pay federal income taxes when I graduate. I am used to getting all the money back that are withheld from me. Can you tell me how I can continue doing this?

PROFESSOR: Well, the only way really is to file a fraudulent tax return which I would not recommend doing. Taxes are a fact of life and you will be paying them.

S: Can you explain taxes to me?

P: I can explain most of it in about a year, so I will have to give you the broad parameters of the situation that you can expect to have.

S: Forget it, I will just have a tax preparer do my tax return after I graduate.

P: That has its positive points and its negative points. You will have a pretty basic return so if you go to a tax preparation service, it will most likely cost you in the $100–$200 range. If you have a basic return for a number of years, you could do it yourself and save some money.

S: I will use tax software then.

P: This will give you an accurate return if you input everything correctly, but I would have to strongly recommend you take the federal taxation course offered at the college. In my opinion, this course will pay for itself over the years.

S: No way, I am not going in there with a bunch of number crunching accountants.

P: Actually, many accountants are significantly involved in operations and business decision making in their companies and in public accounting, when providing advice to their clients. But this discussion is taking us away from the topic at hand. I can tell you that one of the best students that I ever had in taxes was a classics major.

S: How could a classics major do well in a taxation course?

P: Because she thought logically and continually asked questions when she did not follow the topic.

S: The rest of the class must have been bothered by this.

P: Actually no, she was asking the questions they should have been asking so she was doing everyone else a favor.

S: Okay, I'll think about it, but what should I expect to pay in taxes in my first full year after graduation? I am planning on a salary of $50,000 and want to have a good time and may consider saving a little bit also. I won't be married for at least 5 years.

P: Let's assume you donate $3,000 to your employer's 401K plan (remember because of the power of compound interest, you want to start as early as possible) because that maximizes the employer's match. I'll do the calculations based on the new rates for 2018.

S: What do you mean by "that maximizes the employer's match?"

P: Let's focus on taxes now and I'll discuss 401K plans later. With a $50,000 salary, you will pay $3,100 (6.2 percent) in Social Security (SS) taxes and $725 (1.45 percent) in Medicare taxes. Your federal taxable income will be calculated as follows:

Earned Income	$50,000
Less: 401K Contribution	($3,000)
Adjusted Gross Income	$47,000
Less: Standard Deduction	($12,000)
Taxable Income	$35,000

This would put you in the 12 percent tax bracket so your taxes would be approximately $4,010.

S: What do you mean the 12 percent tax bracket?

P: This is your marginal tax rate which is the federal rate that you pay on each additional dollar earned.

S: Professor, I am struggling with tax brackets, marginal tax rate... give me a break here.

P: Don't worry, you will understand this all shortly. There are seven brackets which I will show to you. There are actually four tax tables depending on your filing status; I will use "single" since that is your current status. Remember the taxable income above is the key. When you actually do your taxes, you will use a tax table but the tax schedule below illustrates the concept.

TAXABLE INCOME RANGE	FEDERAL TAX DUE
$0–$9,525	10% of Taxable Income
$9,526–$38,700	$953 + 12% of excess
$38,701–$82,500	$4,454 + 22% of excess
$82,501–$157,500	$14,090 + 24% of excess
$157,501–$200,000	$32,090 + 32% of excess
$200,001–$500,000	$45,690 + 35% of excess
$500,001 and beyond	$150,690 + 37% of excess

S: This is all Greek to me. And I thought there was supposed to be tax simplification which would save me a lot of money!

P: It is Greek to a lot of people but let's look at it this way. Remember your taxable income is $35,000 so your tax due is $953+ (12%*($35,000 - $9,526)) = $4,010. As for saving you money, your federal income tax would have been $1,014 higher last year.

S: Okay, I am starting to understand. So for this marginal tax rate, as my taxable income increases, I need to pay 12 percent of the increase to the federal government.

P: That is true for the next $3,700 of taxable income and then you will move into the 22 percent tax bracket, so for every additional dollar earned, Uncle Sam will get 22 cents.

S: You've lost me again.

P: Okay, can you agree that you are in the range or bracket that goes from $9,526–$38,700?

S: Yes, we already discussed this.

P: What is the next range or bracket?

S: $38,701–$82,500, oh boy, I see the 22 percent of excess. I am there with another $3,700.

P: That does sound familiar.

S: I see the calculation, but that is not fair. Why should the federal government get 22 cents of every additional dollar I earn, and what was it before taxes were just reduced?

P: A topic for another day. These are the facts of the situation. As for what it was before taxes were reduced, you would have been paying 3 cents more or 25 cents on every extra dollar.

Now, you will also most likely pay state income taxes. There are seven states that do not have an income tax and two states (New Hampshire and Tennessee) which do not tax income from your job ("earned income"), but do tax interest and dividends.

S: I am assuming all states calculate taxable income the same as above.

P: Sorry but there would be 43 different calculations and the marginal tax rates differ significantly by state. For the sake of argument, let's assume you live in one of the 41 states that does tax your income from your job ("earned income"); we'll assume your state has a marginal tax rate of 4 percent.

S: Wait a minute! Does this mean I am paying 26 cents on each additional dollar earned once I get to the 22 percent bracket.

P: You are really starting to understand this. At a 22 percent marginal tax rate, when you also factor in Social Security and Medicare, and state income taxes, approximately 34 cents of each additional dollar you earn is going to pay taxes. I may be further confusing the issue but remember the tax schedule we just reviewed? While you are paying Social Security and Medicare taxes on every dollar earned, federal taxes don't start until your taxable income exceeds $12,000 (the standard deduction). Notice then your marginal rate becomes 10 percent, increases to 12 percent and finally to the 22 percent we have discussed.

S: Yikes! What about all these write-offs that I hear about that can save me money? I saw a *Seinfeld* episode where Kramer said everything is a write-off.

P: You are probably referring to itemized deductions and I would not use Kramer as a tax expert. Before the recent tax changes, approximately 30 percent of taxpayers were able to itemize deductions, now approximately 10 percent of taxpayers get to itemize deductions. If you buy a house and are single, you will most likely be able to itemize deductions. If you buy a house and are married, you have a possibility of itemizing deductions.

S: How do you get to itemize deductions?

P: Well, remember that $12,000 I deducted in figuring your taxes?

S: I do.

P: That is the standard deduction for single individuals. If you are married, you should be filing jointly and your standard deduction becomes $24,000. If you have itemized deductions that exceed those levels, then you can take the higher amount of the itemized deductions.

S: Why did you keep bringing up owning a house?

P: Well, in most cases, only people owning houses with significant mortgage interest will be itemizing. With a house, you will have mortgage interest. There are limits there but no need for you to worry about those for years.

S: What is mortgage interest?

P: The interest you pay on the money you have borrowed to buy a house.

S: Well I am paying state income taxes so I get to deduct those right?

P: Using the assumed rate that we discussed of 4 percent and assuming the state in which you work uses the exact same taxable income formula as the federal government, you would pay approximately $1,400 ($35,000 * 4%) in state income taxes. You will most likely not have enough other deductions to be able to itemize.

S: What can be itemized?

P: The most applicable to you are mortgage interest, property taxes, state income taxes, and charitable contributions. If the sum of your allowable itemized deduction is greater than your standard deduction, you will itemize deductions. However, the sum of property taxes, state income taxes, and city income taxes (if you live in New York or another large city that taxes income) is limited to a maximum of $10,000.

S: This is tax simplification?

P: Funny, I just read an article where a CPA [certified public accountant] said, "I hate to be flip but this is going to be an accountant's retirement act." (Rapoport, 2017) That tax course will always be relevant.

S: So say I am married and we have itemized deductions of $28,000, we get to deduct the $28,000?

P: You got it now but let's say you are in the 22 percent marginal tax bracket. What is the real benefit of $28,000 in itemized deductions?

S: Don't insult me, it is $6,160 ($28,000 * 22%).

P: Do me a favor and think this one through again while factoring in the standard deduction.

S: Wow, did I blow that. We itemize deductions so we don't get the standard deduction so we would have had $24,000 but instead got $28,000, or $4,000 more, so the real benefit to us of $28,000 of itemized deductions is $880 ($4,000 * 22%). That doesn't seem right.

P: Well, this is where tax planning comes into play. Let's say you and your spouse had significant charitable contributions of $8,000 to get you to the $28,000.

S: I hope we can donate that much.

P: I certainly hope so also but it is just to illustrate the point. If you can make $16,000 in deductions every other year, what does that do to your itemized deductions, with everything else being equal?

S: Well, they would change to $36,000 in one year and $20,000 in another year.

P: What would be your deduction in the year in which they are $20,000?

S: Well then we would take the standard deduction of $24,000.

P: So under those two scenarios, what are your total deductions for the two years combined?

S: Well shifting the $8,000 of contributions from one year into another gets you $36,000 one year and $24,000 another year for a total of $60,000. Not shifting the $8,000 gets you $28,000 in both years for $56,000. Big deal, I save 22 percent of $4,000, or $880.

P: I agree, it is not a big deal but it illustrates the fact that tax planning can save you money. If we are talking large numbers, there are opportunities there. Never let the tax factors drive the decision, but they can always be considered.

S: Are there any basic rules to remember?

P: The simplest basic rule is the philosophy of taxation. Everything is taxable unless specifically excluded, and nothing is deductible unless specifically authorized. With experience, and a tax course which you can take here at the college as one of your electives, you will learn and understand the basics.

S: I am starting to think I will at least consider taking the tax course. Any other potential advantages?

P: Absolutely. Anyone can mathematically do their taxes, but the key is knowing the potential tax consequences before making decisions that can significantly impact your taxes.

S: "Huh?"

P: Let me give you a very simplistic example. You want to give your favorite organization $2,500 in December. You are closing on a house in January which will finally allow you to itemize deductions. Assuming you are in the 22 percent tax bracket (i.e. marginal tax rate), if you wait until January to give the $2,500, you will have $550 in tax savings because charitable contributions are an itemized deduction.

S: This is scary, I am starting to understand this. Are there any deductions that I might have if I don't itemize deductions?

P: If you pay student loan interest. This is not an itemized deduction which reduces taxable income, but is more valuable because it is deducted in getting to adjusted gross income. Thus you benefit from it even if you don't itemize deductions. Previously you were able to benefit from moving expenses if you were relocating a significant difference in miles to a new job, but that was eliminated so I will only go into the student loan interest.

S: With my basic knowledge of taxation, there has to be a catch here.

P: You are catching on fast, the maximum you can deduct in a year is $2,500. The amount you can deduct phases out (reduces) as your Adjusted Gross Income (AGI) is between $65,000–$80,000.

S: Explain this one.

P: If your AGI is $72,500 (halfway between $65,000 and $80,000), you will lose 50 percent of the deduction and only be able to deduct $1,250 even if you paid $4,000 in student loan interest (and I hope you won't be paying that much). Once your AGI is $80,000, you have no deduction for student loan interest.

S: Do these phase-outs exist in other areas?

P: More than you would care to know.

S: But I can learn many of them in the tax course. No need to reply here.

S: Any other general rules of thumb?

P: I'll just give you two for now to avoid information overload. First, a credit is worth more than a deduction; second, long-term capital gains and dividends are taxed at preferential tax rates.

S: Can you explain here?

P: Sure. Your parents, if they were paying a significant amount of tuition, were most likely taking a $2,500 credit from their tax return for the last three or four years. They would calculate their taxable income, their taxes, and then reduce the taxes by $2,500.

Remember the $2,500 student loan interest deduction being worth $550 (deduction * marginal tax rate); well the $2,500 credit is worth $2,500 and guess what...there is a phase-out associated with this credit.

When we get to investments, I will tell you about capital gains, dividends, and the associated preferential tax rates.

S: I am at information overload. Any last advice.

P: Just the forms for now. Form 1040EZ is the easiest, but you can't use that if you have student loan interest deductible (this is just one example) so you can use Form 1040A. Once you are itemizing deductions (or other factors have arisen) you will itemize deductions on Schedule A and file Form 1040. I do recommend though to anyone I speak with to use Form 1040 (unless you are paying a preparer) because it will give you an idea of the potential deductions available to you now or in the future. The other forms don't necessarily do that. All three forms will get you to the same amount owed.

S: I am going to register for the tax course now. With all these taxes, how am I going to have the fun I was planning on having?

P: Two responses to that. The tax course is your best idea yet. It will be tough and you may be cursing me during the semester but, as I told you, it will pay for itself. Secondly, remember the principles we discussed in budgeting. You can do more than you think now if you budget and spend your money wisely.

Can I tell you one last piece of information you will find interesting?

S: I'm scared to say yes.

P: Well, most of the recent tax changes expire at the end of 2025, meaning if Congress doesn't do anything before then, we go back to the old rules.

S: You're kidding me right?

P: I wish I was.

BANKING

STUDENT: At this time, I do my banking online and have a savings account. The savings account was set up by my parents years ago; the online banking was set up when I started college. I hate to admit it, but my online banking experience consists of my parents periodically putting money in there for me and me withdrawing it when I need cash.

PROFESSOR: Do you balance your online banking information?

S: What do you mean by balance? It is always telling me the current balance.

P: Yes, I understand that, but if the bank were to make a mistake and put money in there that is not yours or charges your account for fees or a withdrawal that was not yours, would you be able to determine that?

S: Banks would not make these types of mistakes.

P: Mistakes happen everywhere, which is why you need to develop good cash management skills.

S: Okay, tell me something about banks.

P: There are many different types of banks; the differences between the types were far greater when I was going through school, but they have narrowed considerably over the years.

S: Did they have banks when you were going through school?

P: I'll pretend I didn't hear that comment and you just lost two strokes on the course.

Generally the type providing the most services, particularly for businesses, are commercial banks. These are the bigger banks such as JP Morgan, Wells Fargo, et cetera.

There are savings and loan associations. Previously these were focused on providing mortgages, however they have expanded their offerings over the years.

S: Can we go through what is involved with a mortgage?

P: For sure, but at a later time. Let's focus on you putting away some of your money once you start earning it, which will help you get a mortgage later.

There are mutual or cooperative savings banks which are owned by the depositors. Ironically, these are most prevalent in the northeast and not in many other areas of the country.

There are also credit unions which are nonprofit entities.

S: Hold it there, what is an entity?

P: Just a synonym for a business and it can be either a for-profit business or a not-for-profit business.

Now, going back to credit unions, previously you had to have a common affiliation or be part of a specific group to be a member of a credit union. That has pretty much been changed so anyone can join any credit union. Credit unions have an advantage over other types of banks as they are established as non-profits, which means they pay no federal income taxes and their "earnings" are continually reinvested in the business. You can often find lower loan rates and higher savings rates at a credit union.

S: How are my savings protected?

P: You want to be sure that any bank you use is covered by the FDIC, the Federal Depositors Insurance Corporation. This provides protection up to $250,000 per account in a bank. I am hoping some day you will need to worry about having to put money in a second bank because some day you are close to exceeding the limit.

For a credit union, make sure the entity you are looking at is a member of the National Credit Union Association. This protects your money similar to how the FDIC does for banks.

S: So what are they going to pay me for allowing them to hold my money?

P: Not much I'm afraid. Let's go through this rate sheet from Piscataqua Savings Bank in Portsmouth, New Hampshire. It is a one branch mutual savings bank, meaning it has one location and is owned by its depositors. So if you have your money there, you are an owner.

S: Why would I want to deal with a bank that only has one branch?

P: I'll get into considerations later with respect to a larger bank or a smaller bank. I can only tell you from experience that this is a great bank with which to deal.

I am giving you a rate sheet here. Now keep in mind that I printed this off for you quite some time ago. The rates may have changed since then but the concepts, which is what I want you understand, have not. Let's look at the second page first which has the section "Savings and Checking Accounts." You are probably looking at a passbook or statement savings account which needs $10 to open and $100 to earn interest. Interest rates are historically very low right now so the rate is 0.2 percent and the annual percentage yield is 0.2 percent.

SAVINGS AND CHECKING ACCOUNTS

ACCOUNT PRODUCT NAME	MINIMUM OPENING DEPOSIT	MINIMUM BALANCE TO EARN APY	INTEREST RATE	APY**
Passbook/Statement Savings All balances. The interest rate and annual percentage yield may change after account opening.	$10.00	$100.00	0.20%	0.20%
Christmas/Vacation Clubs All balances. The interest rate and annual percentage yield may change after account opening.	$1.00	$1.00	0.20%	0.20%
Checking Account All balances. The interest rate and annual percentage yield may change after account opening. Fees could reduce earnings on the account	$100.00	$1.00	0.05%	0.05%

*The interest rate and annual percentage yield may change after account opening
**APY: Annual Percentage Yield

SAVINGS AND CHECKING ACCOUNTS

Health Savings Account Up to $2.499.99*	$100.00	$1.00	0.20%	0.20%
Health Savings Account Balances of $2,500.00 - $9,999.99*	$100.00	$2,500.00	0.45%	0.45%
Health Savings Account Balances of $10,000.00 and over*	$100.00	$10,000.00	0.70%	0.70%

*The interest rate and annual percentage yield may change after account opening
**APY: Annual Percentage Yield

S: What does all that mean?

P: For most of these accounts, you will see that the interest Rate and annual percentage yield (APY) are the same. This is primarily because interest rates are so low. If interest rates are higher and compounding occurs more frequently than annually, the APY will be greater than the interest rate. As you begin to compare banks with respect to account returns, the APY is your common basis of comparison.

S: So if I keep $1,000 in there for a year, how much do I earn?

P: $2 ($1,000 * .002)

S: You're kidding me right? Why do I even want to talk about this?

P: Because this is your starting point and you should have an account. In due course, as you accumulate money, there are all sorts of options as to where you put your money. Always remember the risk versus reward factor: the greater the potential return, the higher the risk, and vice versa. You can lose money on a savings account only in very unusual circumstances that are of no concern to you.

Christmas/Vacation Clubs are where people put away money each week to cash out just before Christmas.

A checking account allows you to write checks to pay your bills. We'll talk about checking account considerations later, but note that the rate is 25 percent of the rate for a passbook account; this rate will always be lower than a passbook account.

We are not going to worry about Health Savings Accounts now.

Let's take a look at certificate of deposits (generally known as "CDs"). Do me a favor, take a look at the rate sheet for a couple of minutes and let me know if you notice anything.

CERTIFICATES OF DEPOSIT

ACCOUNT PRODUCT NAME	MINIMUM OPENING DEPOSIT	MINIMUM BALANCE TO EARN APY	INTEREST RATE	APY**
3-Month*	$2,500.00	$2,500.00	0.40%	0.40%
6-Month* Up to $49,999.99	$2,500.00	$2,500.00	0.50%	0.50%

All of the above fixed rate Certificates of Deposit are available within an IRA plan. For IRA plans, the minimum opening deposit is $500.00
* A penalty may be imposed for early withdrawal. Fees could reduce the earnings on the account
** APY: Annual Percentage Yield

CERTIFICATES OF DEPOSIT

6-Month* $50,000.00 and over	$50,000.00	$50,000.00	0.50%	0.50%
9-Month* up to $49,999.99	$500.00	$500.00	0.50%	0.50%
9-Month* $50,000.00 and over	$50,000.00	$50,000.00	0.50%	0.50%
1-Year* up to $49,999.99	$500.00	$500.00	1.09%	1.10%
1-Year* $50,000.00 and over	$50,000.00	$50,000.00	1.09%	1.10%
1 ½-Year* up to $49,999.99	$500.00	$500.00	1.14%	1.15%
1 ½-Year* $50,000.00 and over	$50,000.00	$50,000.00	1.14%	1.15%
2-Year* up to $49,999.99	$500.00	$500.00	1.24%	1.25%
2-Year* $50,000.00 and over	$50,000.00	$50,000.00	1.24%	1.25%
3-Year* up to $49,999.99	$500.00	$500.00	1.49%	1.50%
3-Year* $50,000.00 and over	$50,000.00	$50,000.00	1.49%	1.50%
5-YR CD* $500.00 and over	$500.00	$500.00	2.13%	2.15%

All of the above fixed rate Certificates of Deposit are available within an IRA plan. For IRA plans, the minimum opening deposit is $500.00
* A penalty may be imposed for early withdrawal. Fees could reduce the earnings on the account
** APY: Annual Percentage Yield

S: Well, under the account product name, the longer the period of time is, the higher the APY is.

P: Now you are learning how to look at things.

S: But what is a CD?

P: A CD is an account where you guarantee the bank that you will keep the deposited amount with them for a specific period of time. Because you are willing to keep it with them for a specific period of time, they are willing to pay you a better rate than on a savings account. The longer you will keep it with them, the higher the rate they are willing to pay you.

You will notice also that some time periods are the same, but one time period has "up to $49,999.99" and another time period has $50,000 and up.

S: Yes, I was wondering about that.

P: There is no difference here in rates, but frequently banks will pay higher rates on more dollars for the same length of time.

S: What if I think I can put the money away for a certain period of time, but things change? How do I go about getting my money?

P: That is what the asterisk (*) on each CD is referencing. Generally a bank charges three months interest for an early withdrawal, so if you have had the money there for longer than three months, you walk away with more than you started, just not as much as you hoped when you invested the money.

If you take it out before three months are over, you will walk away with less money than you originally invested.

S: That doesn't seem fair.

P: Well, you made a deal with the bank where they were willing to pay you more and the bank invests that money elsewhere. If you are budgeting properly as we have discussed, this situation should only happen if some completely unforeseen event occurs.

IRAs are retirement accounts. We won't worry about those now. Let's look at money market accounts.

IRAs				
ACCOUNT PRODUCT NAME	MINIMUM OPENING DEPOSIT	MINIMUM BALANCE TO EARN APY	INTEREST RATE	APY**
1-1/2 Year Variable IRA* All balances. The interest rate and annual percentage yield may change after account opening.	$10.00	$10.00	0.45%	0.45%

*The interest rate and annual percentage yield may change after account opening
**APY: Annual Percentage Yield

MONEY MARKET

ACCOUNT PRODUCT NAME	MINIMUM OPENING DEPOSIT	MINIMUM BALANCE TO EARN APY	INTEREST RATE	APY**
Balances up to $2,499.99*	$2,500.00	$1.00	0.05%	0.05%
Balances of $2,500.00 - $49,999.99*	$2,500.00	$2,500.00	0.30%	0.30%
Balances of $50,000.00 and over*	$2,500.00	$50,000.00	0.30%	0.30%
Premier Money Market - $25,000.00 - $49,999.99*	$25,000.00	$25,000.00	0.30%	0.30%
Premier Money Market - $50,000.00 - $99,999.99*	$25,000.00	$50,000.00	0.75%	0.75%
Premier Money Market - $100,000.00 - $250,000.00*	$25,000.00	$100,000.00	0.75%	0.75%

*The interest rate and annual percentage yield may change after account opening
**APY: Annual Percentage Yield
Fees could reduce the earnings on this account

With the money market account illustrated here, as you can see, the more you have on deposit, the higher the rate you can earn which is the standard feature at all banks. With the money market accounts featured here, you can make up to six withdrawals a month (and there are ways the number can be increased) so the money is a bit more flexible than a CD.

S: And because of this flexibility these accounts generally pay lower rates than CDs?

P: You are a fast learner. As you can see in all the topics we have discussed so far, there are generally various options for each topic. My job is to have you understand the differences and options so you can ask the right questions when they count.

S: What about stocks, bonds, mutual funds, the exciting stuff?

P: We'll get to those later, let's go back to the section we started with and look at a checking account.

S: I don't ever see myself writing checks.

P: Maybe not but if you have kids and they are involved in youth sports, activities, et cetera, checks are still a very popular payment method. Also, you may be walking by that Salvation Army kettle just before Christmas and haven't had change all year. Your debit card will do you no good, but you can always slide a check into that kettle.

S: You already told me that checking accounts pay a lower interest rate than savings accounts. Why is that?

P: Because the money is in and out far more quickly than a savings account and the bank has more costs associated with a checking account.

S: Okay, my parents have given me enough checks to give to groups I have joined over the years so I know how they work.

P: Do you know how to balance a checking account?

S: I can't say that I do. Why do I need to balance a checking account?

P: To make sure you have money in there to cover a check when you write one. If you "bounce" a check (you did not have enough money in the account to cover the amount written), a bank will probably have a fee of $20 or so and the company or group will charge you a fee of $20 or so. If it was to your friend, he/she may not charge you a fee, but that is embarrassing. Bounce a few checks and it gets expensive.

S: So how do I balance a checking account?

P: I'll give you a very simplistic example, but the concept is the same no matter how much activity has occurred. You are comparing what has happened in your checking account since you balanced last month to what has happened in your checkbook. Let's say you had a $5 balance in your account, you deposited $500 mid-month and $500 after 2 p.m. on the last Friday of the month. During the month, you wrote two checks after the middle of the month, one for $200 and one for $250.

S: So what is so difficult about this? I don't even need a calculator. $5 + $500 + $500 -$200 - $250 = $555.

P: You are correct with the math, but now you get your bank statement and your balance is $305.

S: How can that be?

P: Well we need to look at what has happened on the bank statement. I see the following:

$5 + $500 - $200 = $305

S: Where is my second deposit of $500? Have I been ripped off?

P: Not at all, you have probably noticed the notice in the bank that deposits made after 2 p.m. are processed the next business day.

S: You're right, but I never paid attention to it.

P: Well in this case, if you made the deposit after 2 p.m. on the last Friday of the month and the month ends that day, Saturday or Sunday, then your deposit will be credited on the first business day of the next month. In accounting terms, it is a "deposit in transit."

S: You're not going to start teaching me accounting are you? I want no part of that.

P: Not at all, but if you ever think you might start your own business, I think you are making a mistake if you don't take accounting. Now back to the bank statement, anything else missing?

S: Yes, the check I wrote for $250 is not there.

P: Good catch, that check has not been cashed as of month end by the person you gave it to, so it is an outstanding check (not the same as a great check in hockey). So the bank reconciliation is as follows:

Balance per bank $305 + Deposit in Transit $500 - Outstanding Checks $250 = $555 which coincidentally enough is the balance per books.

S: That's not bad. What else can happen?

P: The most common things would be if the bank gives you interest during the month, you will add it to your checkbook balance; if the bank charges you a fee during the month, you subtract it from your checkbook balance. Again, it is reviewing what is on one set of records that is not on the other. The other area where people make a mistake is if an outstanding check at the end of one month has not been cashed in the next month, it remains an outstanding check to be subtracted from the bank balance. As long as a check remains outstanding, it factors into each month's reconciliation.

S: I may start my own business someday. Why do you think it is wise to take accounting?

P: Because it will help you to understand what is happening in your business better. The numbers are not good or bad by themselves; they only portray what is happening in the business and allow you to ask the right questions to hopefully allow you to make the right strategic moves. Yes, debits and credits are tough, but you'd be surprised by the business concepts discussed. And, of course, you better be able to do, or review, a bank reconciliation.

S: Why is that?

P: Sad to say, I could give you an article a week about a significant embezzlement of funds by a bookkeeper or an accountant. It can be scary how much can be stolen in a small business if the owner completely turns over all financial matters to one person. When you read about most of them, if the owner had been reviewing a bank reconciliation in any way, shape or form, it should have been detected well before becoming as large as it did.

S: Any other thoughts on banks?

P: Yes, in my opinion, the average person is much better off dealing with a small local bank or credit union than a large regional or national bank. The level of customer service I have found is unmatched. When I have made a couple of mistakes, solutions were able to be found immediately because the bank knew me and accepted my explanation in good faith. If I were dealing with a larger bank, I fear I would be still trying to figure out what option to press on the phone system.

I found a large bank reordering withdrawals on a debit card that had been overcharged (not mine) in order to maximize their charges. What they did led to $175 in fees for what should have been a $35 fee. It was outright theft and they were later called to task in a lawsuit.

S: Explain that one to me.

P: That is a long story. Anyone reading this discussion is ready to move on.

CREDIT BASICS

STUDENT: Well, based on what you have told me so far, it looks like I will need to be borrowing some money when I graduate, if not before then.

PROFESSOR: If you have student loans, you are currently borrowing. Student loans are a topic best discussed at a later time since they come in many different forms. I'll discuss the basic types of credit with you and, between our discussion here and our discussion to follow on FICO scores, you'll have enough knowledge to make good borrowing decisions.

S: Let's start off with some of the types of credit that may be available to me.

P: Sure, but first understand that there are two general groupings of credit: open-end and closed-end.

S: Is this going to be as confusing as taxes?

P: We only touched the tip of the tax iceberg and I assure you that credit will not be as confusing as taxes. That said, pay attention because sometimes bad credit decisions are very costly mistakes. With open-end credit, there is generally a minimum required payment each month, but there is no definitive payoff date for the loan. You can borrow up to a predetermined amount and as long as you are making the minimum payments, you are all set.

S: Are you recommending to make the minimum payments each month?

P: My recommendation is completely different, but we'll get to that in due course.. With closed-end credit, you have a fixed payment to be made each month and there is a predetermined date at which the loan will be paid (or possibly refinanced).

S: So what represents open-end credit and what represents closed-end credit?

P: Open-end credit is credit cards whether they are bank issued or department store issued. Also when you own a home, a home equity line of credit is somewhat open-end credit. Generally only the interest is payable each month, but there is a definitive date at which the entire amount needs to be paid.

S: I've been thinking of getting a credit card; do you recommend I do so?

P: It depends on your maturity. I would strongly recommend getting one if you have the discipline to only use it for necessity purchases for which you could have otherwise paid cash or for a true emergency.

S: Are you insulting me, questioning my maturity?

P: Not intentionally, I am only telling you from experience that I have seen many students that I thought were more mature than you mishandle credit cards and create financial problems for themselves. At the same time, I have seen students I thought less mature than you who have handled credit cards flawlessly. I know for certain that I can't pre-judge a student's financial maturity.

S: What are my risks with credit cards?

P: Quite significant, firstly the interest rates are very high which can significantly increase your purchasing costs. Secondly, poor use of credit cards can put you in a financial hole that is tough from which to recover; and thirdly, misused credit cards will negatively impact your FICO score which can lead to costing you tens of thousands of dollars over your lifetime. We'll discuss FICO scores next.

S: Give me an example of immediate problems.

P: Let's say you need that $400 game player so you can get ready for your physically demanding eSports competition. If you put the game on your credit card and only pay what is generally the required minimum payment of 2 percent and an interest rate of 18 percent (probably too low), you'll finish paying that off in month 94 (7 years and 10 months) and pay $344.89 in interest. You have almost doubled the cost of your purchase (and I have used a conservative calculation as I have used a consistent $8 per month).

S: What if I want to skip a month?

P: No problem, the non-payment fee generally runs a mere $39.

S: What if I need cash?

P: Get a cash advance and the interest starts accruing right away and it will be at a higher rate than 18 percent. Even if you have paid all your bills on time up to that point, any purchases that have been made in the current period will now start accruing interest.

S: So when do you recommend students get a credit card?

P: When they are financially mature and only use it to purchase necessities or have an emergency requiring it. You want to pay the full balance back each month. When you can't, pay as much as possible and put no further charges on the card. Whatever you do, always make a payment each month. If you remember our discussion of the power of compound interest, it is now working against you in reverse.

S: What about store credit cards which offer an immediate discount?

P: I would never touch them. These generally carry high rates and can be punitive. They can do a lot of harm to your FICO score if not handled properly.

S: I'm scared to borrow now. What about when I need to buy a car?

P: No need to be scared if you handle all your credit cards properly and I would recommend no more than two after you have a job. The rate you pay on your car loan is significantly impacted by your FICO score which is, of course, impacted by how you handle credit.

Remember, you will most likely have a fixed payment each month for a car. Part of each payment is interest and the remainder goes to paying down your loan balance. The less that is going to interest gives you more buying power for a better car. We'll talk about car loans later when we discuss buying a car.

S: Is there any specific credit card you would recommend?

P: I have learned from my students in this case. I had always recommended a Discover Card for them because there is no annual fee, and then they told me about the Discover It Card which comes with three major benefits: it will give you $20 cash back once per year if you get a 3.0 GPA or higher; it gives you a 2 percent cash back reward on gas and restaurant purchases; and at the end of the first year, Discover will match the cash back you have earned. ("Discover It Chrome Card," n.d.) That said, after six months, the annual interest rate can vary between 13.99 percent and 22.99 percent.

S: Compounding in reverse. I understand this concept well now. Also, remember I go to Saint A's which is well known by students here, and at other schools, as Saint C's because of a strict grading policy so forget the 3.0. What about buying a house?

P: The school, as Father Jonathan mentioned at commencement a few years ago, is actually now Saint B's based on current grade point averages so the 3.0 is a realistic number if you study more. We'll discuss buying a house later.

S: You like to discuss many things at a later time.

P: Absolutely. There are many areas within personal finance, so I like to partition them as best I can and when relevant, explain how they interrelate because they certainly do so. We'll keep the discussion to small segments so you can always come back to a specific segment at a later time when needed.

S: Any last comments with respect to credit?

P: Sure, I will give you a couple of caveats. I did read an article about young people who have accumulated many credit cards to take advantage of the all the incentives like 60,000 air miles, free hotel nights, et cetera that cards offer. One young couple had 40. (Copeland, 2017) Definitely a risky gamble that I would not recommend to most, but some people can pull it off.

The other was related to a couple that uses four credit cards with different cash back incentives. For gas purchases, they use the best gas card which gets them 5 percent back. For groceries, they use the best card and get 6 percent back; the best for restaurants and travel gets them 3 percent and then they have a 2 percent card for everything else. (Martin, 2017) I'll have to say I was quite impressed.

S: So you are telling me I should have four credit cards.

P: For most, I recommend no more than two. It takes great discipline to use that four-card system and I can see many people digging a great hole for themselves.

S: I'm ready to discuss this FICO score you have been mentioning.

P: Coincidentally I am ready to discuss your adult GPA.

A GUIDE TO YOUR ADULT GPA

STUDENT: What is your adult GPA?

PROFESSOR: Your adult GPA is your FICO score which measures your past history regarding debt.

S: When does it start counting?

P: Six months after you begin incurring debt.

S: What do you mean by incurring?

P: It means you have used credit cards and hopefully have been paying them in full each period they are due.

S: When can you get a credit card?

P: You can get one as you are 21. Individuals under 21 are able to get one if their parents are willing to co-sign for him/her. Please be aware that I am not recommending that to any parents. I am just telling you the options.

S: Why should I get one now?

P: To prove you can handle debt responsibly and start to build your credit history.

S: Why should I start to build my credit history now?

P: Think of it as a sports game. Most professionals agree it is easier to play with the lead rather than trying to come from behind. It doesn't matter what the sport is.

S: I'm struggling to think of credit history as a sports game.

P: Actually, many things in the finance area are like sports. If you handle the credit card properly, you will be in front; if you mishandle it, you may be playing catch up for quite some time. Let's say the credit card company starts you off with a limit of $300; not bad, even with inflation. You can do a lot with $300. They only request a minimum payment of $6 per month.

S: I can borrow $300 and only pay $6 per month?

P: Absolutely. As you pay it off, the amount the credit card company requires as the minimum decreases, but I'll use that just to illustrate the concept.

If you pay the $6 per month and assuming your interest rate is a low 18 percent (many cards are higher), it will only take you seven years and 10 months and cost you an extra $259. What's an extra $6 per month when you are paying off student loans years after you graduate?

I hope you can appreciate my sarcasm here. I have seen too many people dig significant financial holes for themselves because each item would only cost them a little more each month. Too many items were purchased and they found themselves deep in debt with high interest costs.

S: I will do my best to remember that. Just asking now, can I borrow any more than the $300?

P: If you establish a payment history, they will normally increase your balance. Let's say they increase it to $1,000.

S: Great, I can borrow another $700.

P: Absolutely…and it will only cost you $14 per month, but I do have to tell you it will take you the same seven years and 10 months to pay back the extra $700 and the total interest charge is $604.

S: No problem. I can get more than one card right, like those couples you mentioned that have 40.

P: Unfortunately, you can get quite a few cards, but again I recommend you not have more than two. If you have a lot of credit cards and miss payments, it could make buying a car in the future a bit more difficult.

S: What does buying a car have to do with these credit cards?

P: Again unfortunately, I have to bore you with the FICO thing.

S: Okay, explain it to me now. You started with FICO, got into sports, got into silly computations about trivial amounts of money; I wish you could stay focused.

P: Okay back to FICO. It is a standardized view of your debt history. Basically, it is a scoreboard as to how you have handled debt. Your FICO score can range from 300 (think of that as flunking) to 850 (an A+).

S: Who cares about how I have handled debt? A car dealer won't know how I have handled debt.

P: Au contraire mon ami. They won't even think about lending to you unless they see your FICO score.

S: Invasion of privacy, they have no right to that!

P: You are absolutely right unless you want to borrow from them; then they have every right in the world.

S: Okay then, no problem. I have always paid off the minimum on time.

P: You are absolutely right but…they will want to be paid off in less than seven years and 10 months; heck, the car might not even last that long and you need slightly more than $300 for the car.

S: Okay, what are we talking about here?

P: Let's say you need to borrow $20,000 to pay the car off over four years. If you look at car dealer ads, in the small print you will see a lot of rates are based on a minimum FICO score of 720. So, based on some figures I have from October 2017 ("Loan Savings Calculator,"n.d.), a 720 FICO score with a 48 month loan will cost you $424 per month. Let's say you decided to have fun and run up some good credit card tabs, miss some payments, et cetera and your credit score is in the 620–659 range, then your monthly payment is $506 per month.

S: What's an extra $82 per month if I had some good times with my friends?

P: Again, pardon my sarcasm but what's a mere $984 per year or $3,936 over the life of the loan? All those pizzas on your credit card tasted good! I should mention to you that you are probably looking at a five year loan, which makes the overall difference a lot larger, not to mention that you will end up "upside down" on the car during the loan.

S: What do you mean "upside down?"

P: That is better left to another day and I'll discuss it when we specifically discuss auto loans. I want to make sure you understand FICO.

S: Okay, I'll bite. What makes up the FICO score?

P: FICO is, as we speak, in a transitional phase, but the basic elements making up your score are: ("What's In Your Credit," n.d.)

Payment History	35%
Amounts Owed	30%
Length of Credit History	15%
Types of Credit in Use	10%
New Credit	10%

Just so you understand, these are the basic elements. They are weighted differently for different people depending on how long they have had credit and a host of other factors.

S: Okay, I'll suffer with the excess payments on the car loan. The damage is done.

P: Actually, not to further depress you, but the car loan is chump change compared to a mortgage.

S: Okay, I'll bite. What's a mortgage?

P: A mortgage is the loan by which the majority of people buy a house. Because it is much larger than a car loan, it will generally be from 15 to 30 years long.

S: Give me an illustration please.

P: My pleasure. I'll just use some illustrative rates I have found for a bank with some of the better rates. ("Mortgage Rates," 2018) Let's say you are looking at a $300,000 mortgage; if your FICO score is 740 or above, you could get 4 percent for a 30 year mortgage which would make your principal (paying down the balance) and interest payments $1,432 per month.

S: I know what's coming, but let's look at it anyways. What if my FICO score is much lower?

P: Well let's say you did have many good times with your friends and you had no trouble reaching for your credit card all the time to entertain, missed some payments, et cetera. You have found yourself with a credit score in the 660–679 range which means 4.5 percent for the same mortgage and your principal and interest payments are $1,520 or another $88 per month.

S: Sad to say, I am starting to understand what you are talking about but...what happened to the 720–850 range you used for the car?

P: A longer time period means more risk for the lender so, to put it in poker terms, the "stakes are raised." The 620–659 we discussed for the car loan may, in some cases, make you ineligible at specific banks.

S: Well I am only going to stay in my first house for 10 years so I can handle the extra $88 per month if I am in the 660–679 range.

P: You can stay there for a month if you want but...based on your 10 years, you will have made an extra $10,560 in payments over that time. Too bad, that would have been a nice chunk of change when making your move, it could have been a good payment towards a car or it could have been invested in the stock market. Based on some data I worked with regarding returns on the Standard & Poor 500 including dividends from 1928–2017 (Damodaran, 2018) , my calculation shows an effective annual return of 9.65 percent. Just using a return of 8 percent and investing the $1,056 for 10 years would return $15,298 to you.

S: Explain the stock market to me.

P: That's a later discussion.

S: I won't worry about the mortgage thing; I will be making so much money after I leave Saint A's that I'll pay cash for the house.

P: I admire your self-confidence and ambition, but I also have to tell you another thing about your FICO score.

S: Let me guess, wherever I work will pay me less if I have a bad credit score. I won't believe that for a minute.

P: Actually, it is more complicated than that. You may never get the job in the first place. Currently, approximately 25 percent of employers check some potential employee's credit history and approximately 6 percent check all applicants . ("Why Employers Check," 2017) My guess is that percentage will only increase over time.

S: What in the world does my credit history have to do with my ability to do my job?

P: Quite a bit actually. Your credit history can be viewed as a measure of your character and integrity, definitely your ability to manage your affairs, and certainly your ability to manage money. Let's say you own a company and are hiring for a key position. Do you want someone in that position that can't manage their own affairs?

S: Any other cheerful news on FICO?

P: Well if you have an overdue library book or parking tickets that have been sent to collection, it is going to negatively impact your FICO score. The big cities are actually sending these to collection and believe it or not, some colleges. In some states, you will pay more for auto and home insurance with a bad FICO score. Again, a bad FICO score says you are a risky investment for any lender. Would you lend money to anyone that might not pay you back?

S: Okay, I get the point. Any other cheerful news on credit cards?

P: Well, not to further depress you, but if you don't pay the minimum or pay on time, you will probably be charged around $39.

S: Just for one day late?

P: They have the right to do that. If you only pay the minimum, every future purchase begins accumulating interest from the date of purchase. So as a rule of thumb, just assume everything you are buying with the card costs you an extra 1.5 percent per month. How much can that possibly add up?

S: Okay, no need to get wise with me. It is sinking in. So…I should avoid a credit card at all cost?

P: It goes back to your financial maturity. Remember you thought I insulted you when we discussed the basics of credit. If you believe that you can properly manage one, a no annual fee card with a low minimum is a good way to get started, but if you don't think you can restrict yourself to only buying necessities and paying it off each month, I would wait.

Remember the FICO factors. If you start establishing a good payment history and building the length of credit history now, the first 80 percent is in your favor. Back to sports terminology, you will be playing with the lead.

S: What is not in my FICO score?

P: Many items. I'll list off the most relevant for you at this point: your race, color, religion, national origin, sex, marital status, age, salary, occupation, title, employer, date employed, employment history, and where you live.

S: How do I find out what's in my credit report?

P: An excellent question. Listen to this one carefully. There are three primary credit reporting agencies which are Experian, Equifax, and TransUnion. By federal law, they need to give you a free credit report once each year. How often should you be checking your credit report?

S: Every four months.

P: And you should do it like clockwork. Identity theft is a major issue where you are guilty until you prove yourself innocent and, even after doing that, it can still be costing you money.

S: What if something is wrong on my credit report?

P: You can contact the credit agency immediately and dispute it. If you are correct, it should be removed.

S: How do I get a good FICO score?

P: There is no magic formula, but the following tips will help:

1. Pay your bills on time. Even if you cannot pay the full amount, make a payment.

2. Never let anything get to a collection agency. Even if you pay off the collection agency, it will remain on your credit report for seven years.

3. Keep balances low. Your score considers your credit utilization rate which is the percentage of available credit you are using. The higher your utilization rate, the more the chances of a hit to your FICO score.

4. Don't open a lot of new credit cards that you don't need.

5. If you are searching for a loan, it will trigger inquiries to your credit report from potential lenders. Try to keep your search focused within a 30-day window as all inquiries will be viewed as a single inquiry rather than multiple inquiries which can impact your score. Your credit history reports inquiries made in the last two years, but the FICO score only considers those made in the last year.

P: Most importantly, never give up on your FICO score. Let's say you have a setback and your FICO score drops dramatically. Always remember that older items count for less so always strive to improve it and it can change significantly as you establish a good payment history and the older items age.

S: So what is the mathematical formula for the FICO score?

P: I'm not sure anyone can tell you that. You may have a better chance of picking every NCAA basketball tournament game right. Let's move on to autos and other loans to make sure you borrow responsibly here and positively impact your FICO score.

AUTO & OTHER LOANS

STUDENT: I hate the idea of debt, but know I will need it to buy a house. Let's discuss mortgage loans and I fully appreciate that I will need to make my mortgage payment each month.

PROFESSOR: That and other costs also which we will discuss later. Before we look at mortgage loans, let's consider other types of loans. We will use the loan sheet from Piscataqua. Other banks will have rate sheets which may differ in form and presentation, but you will easily be able to understand them.

AUTO LOANS				
TYPE	**YEAR**	**TERM**	**APR**	**MONTHLY PAYMENT PER $1,000**
New Car - 80% of purchase price	2017	24	6.500%	$44.55
New Car - 80% of purchase price	2017	36	6.500%	$30.65
New Car - 80% of purchase price	2017	48	6.500%	$23.71

AUTO LOANS

Used Car - 80% of book value or purchase price, which ever is less	2015-2016	24	7.000%	$44.77
Used Car - 80% of book value or purchase price, which ever is less	2015-2016	36	7.000%	$30.88
Used Car - 80% of book value or purchase price, which ever is less	2013-2014	24	7.500%	$45.00
Used Car - 80% of book value or purchase price, which ever is less	2013-2014	36	7.500%	$31.11

UNSECURED PERSONAL LOANS

TYPE	LOAN AMOUNT	TERM	APR	MONTHLY PAYMENT PER $1,000
Minimum	$500.00	12	14.000%	$89.79
Maximum	$5000.00	24	14.000%	$48.01

COLLATERAL LOANS

ACCOUNT TYPE	LOAN AMOUNTS	APR	MONTHLY PAYMENT
Savings Secured - 2% over the Annual Percentage Yield on the account securing the loan rounded up to the next 1/4%	Minimum Amount: $500. Maximum Amount: 100% of account balance.	2.250%	Interest Only or monthly principal and interest
Certificate of Deposit - 2% over the Annual Percentage Yield on the CD securing the loan rounded up to the next 1/4%	Minimum Amount: $500. Maximum Amount: 100% of account balance.	Variable	Interest Only or monthly principal and interest

You're getting pretty good, as I told you that you would, as you discuss more and more topics. Understand the concepts, and the knowledge is transferable to many areas.

Do me a favor, I want to buy a new car for $30,000 and pay for it for four years. I can qualify for the loan. How much do I need to pay upfront for the car, and how much will my monthly payment be?

S: You're kidding me right? I told you I have no interest in being in an accountant.

P: No worries, but I know rather than giving up you are capable of giving me the answer.

S: Let's see here, I see three rows that cover new cars and I see they even give the model year as the current year. I want the third row and see that the APR...what the heck is that? I know I've seen something similar to that acronym.

P: Just think for a minute and let me know.

S: It was back with the savings discussion and it was the APY which I don't remember what it stands for...

P: Annual percentage yield and, more importantly, what did it do?

S: It...allows you a common basis of comparison with respect to savings accounts.

P: So take an educated guess at what APR is when looking at loan rates and tell me what it does.

S: It has to be annual percentage rate, which allows you to compare loans on a common basis.

P: And why would the APR differ on a loan at the same rate between two banks?

S: It has to be because of the frequency of compounding...and you're still not going to make an accountant out of me.

P: Let's continue on with the original question.

S: So if you buy a new 2017 car for $30,000 and want to pay over the course of four years, according to this you would need to put $6,000 down (20 percent) which leaves you borrowing $24,000. It has an APR of 6.5 percent and the monthly payment is $23.71 per thousand. So you are borrowing $24,000 which is 24 $1,000s, so 24 multiplied by $23.71 equals $569.04. Yikes, $569 per month?!

P: Looks like you might want to rethink what you are going to buy for a car.

S: No problem, based on what I know and looking at this, the more time I take to pay, the lower the monthly payment will be. I have heard about car loans out to seven years so I can do even better than the car of my dreams. I am starting to think of myself as a financial genius.

P: I'll withhold comment on that, but just look at that rate schedule and tell me if something sticks out whether it is for a new car or used.

S: Well I notice that used cars carry a higher rate than new cars, the loan rates on older used cars are higher than the loan rates on newer used cars, and based on the many things that we have discussed, I understand the reasoning for that. Also for used cars, if I pay more than book value, they will only loan me 80 percent of book value so I am not borrowing 80 percent of the purchase cost.

P: You are getting very good at reading financial-related information. What else is there?

S: Well, the longest-term rate they will give out is 48 months on a new car and 36 months on a used car. Looks like I will have to go elsewhere to get my seven year loan and the car of my dreams.

P: Sounds more like a nightmare to me. I would never recommend taking a car loan more than four years; if it is going to be more than four years, you need to rethink your make and model purchase.

S: Why is that? I am good to pay it.

P: You probably are, but with a more than four year car loan, you are going to find yourself "upside down" at some point during the loan period.

S: You mentioned this earlier and told me you would explain it so...what is it?

P: It means that at some point, you will owe more on the car than it is worth.

S: Yes, but that is why I have car insurance. If I have an accident and the dollar value of the damage is greater than what the car is worth (it is "totaled" in insurance terms), my insurance takes care of everything...right? I'll just go out, put down a down payment with the insurance money, and start over again.

P: Wrong! If you total the car when its book value is less than the loan amount, what you receive from the insurance company will be less than what you owe on the loan so you will be writing a check to the bank.

S: You need to explain this one to me.

P: Say your car is worth $12,000, the loan balance is $14,000, and you have a $500 deductible.

S: Right, so I will have to pay the deductible of $500.

P: If only that were true. The insurance company is going to write a check to the bank for $11,500 ($12,000 - $500) and then you are going to have to come up with $2,500 to pay off the loan balance. So much for the deposit for your dream car.

S: I don't like where this is going.

P: At least you now have the smarts not to get yourself into this situation.

S: But what about the car ad I always hear? If you bring home $350 per week, you can qualify for up to $30,000 in credit.

P: Do the math and tell me about this deal.

S: Well if you're bringing home $350 a week, you are bringing home a total of $18,200 a year, say $1,000 a month for rent, food, insurance...the math is not working for me.

P: I cringe every time I hear the ad.

S: What is an unsecured personal loan?

P: The bank will give you a loan with nothing more than good faith in your ability to repay it.

S: Why would they do that?

P: If they judge you as a person of good character and you had a good reason for wanting the money, they are willing to take a chance on you.

S: But the rate is 14 percent; you have told me that you are cheap so you would never recommend that.

P: Don't assume anything in the world of finance. When we discuss your FICO score, if you have successfully handled different types of debt, it is a factor in your favor. Length of credit history is also a favorable factor if done properly as we discussed.

Let's say you want to go on a great vacation with your friends that will run you $2,000 which you don't have, but you do have a steady job that you have had for a while and that pays you well. You have dealt with the bank for a while, they know you and like you and are willing to take a shot on you. You borrow the $2,000. How much will you pay back if you borrow it for 12 months?

S: $2,000 times 14 percent equals $280, so I will pay back $2,280.

P: And I thought you were making progress. You did a great job with the car loan, think this one through the same way.

S: I'll try again, I am borrowing two $1,000s so 2 times $89.79 = $179.58 per month for 12 months which is $2,155. Let's see then, it costs me $155 extra over 12 months or $12.92 per month to have a great vacation with my friends. I'm willing to do that, but I don't understand why it is $155 and not $280.

P: Because you are "amortizing" the loan balance. Each payment of $179.58 covers the principal (the $2,000) and interest. When you make your first payment of $179.58, the interest is $23.33 and the principal is $156.25. As your principal balance decreases, the interest decreases. Each subsequent monthly payment breaks down into more principal and less interest being paid.

S: What is this amortization?

P: We'll get into that when we discuss mortgages.

S: What are the collateral loans?

P: It means you are borrowing against money you have deposited in the bank.

S: But why would you do that? Why not just take the money out?

P: Excellent question, it would be a personal matter for the "borrower;" maybe they are afraid of taking the money out and not resaving it, so it forces them to resave it by having to make payments each month (although they can pay just the interest if they wish). There could be any number of personal reasons.

S: On to mortgages now?

P: This discussion went longer than I thought, but I am happy you have a good understanding of car loans, particularly not to take longer than a four year loan.

Our discussion with mortgages will go far longer so we'll have a separate discussion at a later time on those and we will also have a separate discussion on student loans.

S: There has to be a *Seinfeld* episode with loans right?

P: A small segment where a periodic character named Mikey thinks Jerry broke his hands with the trunk of his car because he owes him some money. The better one involving cars involves Jerry renting a car and the insurance coverage on a car. Jerry's explanation of what a reservation means to a car rental employee is very good.

S: As we have discussed financing a car, can we discuss how to go about buying a car?

P: Sounds like a good topic.

CAR BUYING

STUDENT: After I graduate, I want to get myself a car. Based on our discussions, I am guessing you have some opinions on car buying.

PROFESSOR: I am very happy you used "opinions" in that statement. Many of the other topics we have discussed are quite factual. There will always be differences of opinions with respect to the facts, but most of my comments with respect to car buying will be my opinion. In all the areas we discuss, I always recommend speaking to as many people as possible, so you hear many different opinions, and someone will inevitably introduce a topic which has not been discussed before.

S: I have never negotiated anything before. Does that put me at a significant disadvantage?

P: I am guessing you have negotiated more than you can remember over the years. You have undoubtedly negotiated with your parents and friends many times. However, in car buying, you are coming up against a person who most likely has far more experience than you.

Before we go any further, can you let me know if you are thinking about buying a new car or a used car?

S: I don't know. Can we discuss both types of cars?

P: We certainly can, let's discuss a used car first but before we do that, I'd like to give you some general rules of thumb to consider. These rules of thumb are more for new cars but many apply to used cars also. Remember also, that these are just my opinions and you want to get the opinions of many others. For general rules of thumb:

1. Don't be locked into a specific make and model. This puts you at an immediate disadvantage in terms of flexibility. You know those checklists that are in the Sunday paper for the NFL games in terms of which team has the advantage at quarterback, running back, wide receiver, defense, coaching, et cetera. If I were to draw up a similar sheet for car buying, the dealer would have all the checkmarks except for one.

2. Ask immediately about what the dealer administrative fee is, as well as other charges that will occur that are not included in their current sticker price.

3. Don't answer questions about how much you can afford. You can provide a general range for discussion purposes, but you are not fully committed to that range.

4. Try to arrange financing before going to the dealer. The dealer may be able to beat the financing but better to have something in hand before going there. We'll talk later about your options. Make sure you agree the price of any car you are considering, and then discuss the financing because advertised low rates may not be available for all makes and models.

5. Don't discuss a trade-in. You may want to trade in a car but that is a separate negotiation after you have agreed the price. The more factors that are in the equation, the more of an advantage to the dealer. You want each factor to be a separate discussion after the price of the car has been agreed.

6. The rebate is generally the manufacturer rebate and costs the dealer nothing. Advertised rebates are normally reflected in the dealer's price and will be noted as "rebate to dealer."

S: That's a lot of rules of thumb.

P: It certainly is, and many people will give you more. The most important advice I will give you is to bring someone with you that knows cars and knows how to negotiate. You'll be surprised once you start asking around who can do that and hopefully, you'll progress and be able to help someone else in the future.

Now, let's discuss used cars. Choose a few makes and models and then there are four excellent places to go to see price ranges and opinions on the cars in which you are interested. These would be:

Kelly Blue Book: www.kbb.com
Edmunds: www.edmunds.com
NADA Guides: www.nadaguides.com
Consumer Reports: www.consumerreports.org
Another site to consider is www.truecar.com. It is especially good for new cars as it shows what others are paying on average in your area.

S: Is there a favorite that you have?

P: I have always found Consumer Reports to be quite accurate with respect to the price range of used cars and, more importantly, with the used cars to avoid. I am a subscriber and each April they have a complete car edition. I have always found their ranking of the cars I have owned—good and bad—to be very accurate in the assessment of different features. I would never buy a used car that Consumer Report notes to avoid. You can find it in the library.

The most important item in Consumer Reports is a listing of the worst used cars and rankings on 17 different features for each model of the car for the last seven years. Additionally, it gives you a price range for model years for each make and model. It is well worth examining.

S: Where do I go to buy a used car?

P: You have many different options here including, but not limited to:

- A private sales/directly from the owner or representative of the owner (This would include cars potentially available from friends or relatives.)
- A used car dealer (These vary considerably in size and offerings.)
- An auto auction outlet
- A new car dealer
- Some credit unions have repossessed cars which are usually sold on a bid basis with a minimum bid specified.

S: Which is the best?

P: No right answer here. You can get good and bad deals at each location, which is why I always come back to getting help from a friend or relative who is a good negotiator and has a good understanding of cars and the car buying process.

Again, have several makes and models in which you are interested and then start to shop. Word of mouth is very important here to get you started with places where people have already had a favorable experience. Likewise, negative word of mouth will keep you away from unnecessary visits to locations.

Price, service, and warranty coverage will certainly be at the top of your list. Some of the cars you consider (particularly with private sales and credit union auctions) will only come with an implied warranty which says that the car will work as intended. Bear in mind that three months after purchase, your definition of intended may differ from the seller's definition of intended. Litigation to resolve any problems unfortunately may not be justified by the expense and time involved.

S: Are you saying then to avoid private sales and credit union repossessed cars?

P: Not at all. You just need to be aware of all the differences in the choices that you are examining. Personally, I like the idea of paying a trained mechanic in the area of $100 to examine a car you are considering purchasing, however I appreciate that money is tight and it may not be feasible. In this case, hopefully you have a friend who is knowledgeable with respect to cars.

S: Any specifics I should be asking the sales rep?

P: Ask about the history report on the car as most used car dealers have access to Carfax or a similar service. You definitely want to stay away from a car that has had any frame damage, flood damage, or a salvage title in the past.

S: What is a certified pre-owned car (CPO)?

P: CPO cars are usually backed by the manufacturer and over 100 items/features with respect to a CPO car are generally inspected. Again, there are wide variations here. If you are buying from a franchised cars seller (i.e. selling particular models of one or more manufacturers), you'll generally have a 12-month warranty. If you are buying from a used car dealer or elsewhere, the manufacturer may not be behind the certification, and what is involved in the certification can differ significantly.

S: So because the manufacturer is standing behind the car, I should get a CPO car?

P: There are very few certainties in car buying with the exception that a CPO car for the same year make and model will cost you more than a non-certified car. It does not absolutely guarantee that it is the best deal. It is like a multiple choice test with far more answers than A, B, C, or D, and there is no one right answer for everyone. You just need to figure out what are the most important factors regarding the price, car, and coverage for you and figure out which potential seller is most closely meeting your needs.

Be aware that used car dealers will generally only offer the state required warranty period whether it is a CPO or not. In Massachusetts, this is 90 days. In most states it is 30 days. After that, you are on your own.

S: A lot to consider.

P: Yes there is. To add more on your plate, if the car is less than two years old with low mileage, you may still be covered under the original warranty, so check that. Check out the price of an extended warranty and just add that to the cost of the car to see if it is feasible. With all the electronics in cars, repairs are expensive.

S: I like it when there is only one right answer.

P: Welcome to the world of personal finance where there are many good answers and some bad answers. You can only do your due diligence (meaning, a proper review of alternatives) in each area and go with the answer that is best for you.

S: Okay, on to new cars. Is this going to be as confusing?

P: Wherever you have many choices, it will be confusing which is why you identify the four to five key factors for you and focus on those. Actually, much of what we have already discussed remains relevant except now we are focused on new car dealers. As always, I give word of mouth recommendations much more credence here than advertising.

You can find new car reviews in many places, but (my personal bias) again I give the most importance here to Consumer Reports which rates new cars extensively. I would not touch a poorly rated car.

So now you are into the differences between dealers and negotiating down from the MSRP (Manufacturers Suggested Retail Price). It is only for a make and model in great demand (i.e. they can sell more than they have) that you should pay MSRP, and I don't think you will be getting one of these for your first car. So being quite repetitive, bring someone with you that knows how to negotiate and buy a car. I will also give you a couple other rules of thumb here, in addition to those previously discussed:

- Don't give your keys to the dealer. Your car may end up stuck in an area behind other vehicles or your keys may become hard to find.
- Don't put down a down payment. The car will be there for you if you are ready to buy in a short time frame. If you do lose it, there will be a similar buy.
- I will repeat the most important one. Find out all the "add on" costs before negotiating the price of the car.
- Ask for the dealer invoice which is the first pass at what the dealer paid. I'll discuss that further in a bit.

S: A lot to remember, any good car buying stories?

P: Not as much to remember as you think and once you go through the process, you'll be a quick learner. I have had many good car buying stories over the years; I'll share one of them with you. We had the car from the advertisement picked out as the price was good. The car was available, I asked the sales rep what the administrative (admin) fee was and I think at the time it was $288. I told the sales rep, if the dealership would waive the admin fee and I liked the test drive, I would buy it. The sales rep went into the dealership and returned after 10 minutes and said the admin fee would be waived. We took the test drive, went to sign the contract and the $288 was added in the contract. When I told the finance manager that it had been agreed it would be waived, to make a long story short (or at least shorter), the situation led to myself, my wife, and my son in a room with the finance manager, sales manager, and owner all insisting that they would not have waived the admin fee. I asked that the sales rep be brought in and I give him credit for saying that I was told it would be waived. The owner said it would come out of his pay, et cetera. It was a nice dog and pony show for $288. Bottom line, there is no way the rep would have told me that without the okay of management, so he was okay and I saved the $288.

Just as a caveat, another dealership gave me a detailed list of everything covered by the admin fee. As they say in the NFL, upon further review, it was all dealer overhead which is covered in the cost of cars, which then makes it additional profit. If you ever take a cost accounting course, you will know overhead well. There is a dealership in the Seacoast area of New Hampshire which miraculously maintains low prices and a $27 admin fee.

And now back to the dealer invoice, if you request and see the invoice, remember that there is normally a 3 percent hold-back (additional profit for the dealer not reflected on the invoice) and they can earn additional volume rebates depending on how many cars they sell in a month or year.

S: Forget about cost accounting. Are dealers shady characters?

P: Not at all, it is like any profession with its good actors and bad actors with far more good than bad. Hopefully you'll find the good actors.

S: What about leasing a car?

P: Again, many differences of opinion here but I would only recommend leasing a car if you are not driving a lot and want a new car every three years. You are still responsible for maintaining the car, financing it, et cetera and any long road trips may be costly at the end of three years.

S: I don't understand the road trip comment.

P: Nor should you at this point, but car leases come with a maximum number of miles that can be driven over the life of the lease. Thirty thousand and thirty-six thousand are the numbers I have seen for three-year leases (i.e. it will be written as 10K and 12K per year in the advertisement). Any excess mileage incurs an additional cost of anywhere from 15 cents to 25 cents per mile. I would hate to have a few long road trips and have an extra 5,000 miles on the car at the end of the lease. Your available cash for your down payment for your next vehicle just got lower.

Always take the time to read the fine print in any significant deals you are doing.

S: I am thinking of working and living in a big city such as Boston, New York, or Chicago. Any thoughts on the type of car in a big city?

P: If it is a big city with good public transportation, I would not even own a car. The parking and insurance will most likely be too expensive for you and dealing with the traffic would not be worth your time or money. If you can get between any combination of key points with public transportation—taxi, Uber, et cetera—that is the way to go. If you need to drive home or elsewhere outside the city periodically, you can rent a car then. I'll be shocked if you did not find the no car option far cheaper.

Like everything else I tell you, do your homework. Houston is a tremendously large city without a public transportation system like Boston or New York, so you may well need a car in Houston.

S: I am starting to see that doing my homework that is optional now is quite important.

P: Absolutely, but it all fits together and interrelates with many other topics we are discussing. With respect to your "optional" homework, please let your parents know, when they get their tuition bills, that homework is not optional. I am sure they will disagree with your treatment of it as optional.

S: I'll leave that one for another day. One last question: When you were talking about the NFL advantage checklist you said the dealer had all the checks except for one. Just curious, what check is in my favor?

P: The ability to walk away at any time. There are many dealers and hopefully you'll find the right one that gets you as close as possible to the deal you are hoping to land.

AUTO INSURANCE

STUDENT: After I finally buy a car, I guess I will need to get automobile insurance. What can you tell me with respect to auto insurance?

PROFESSOR: Well we can run through basic policy provisions and the various options you have. I'll also discuss what you need to consider as you start to accumulate more assets and perhaps have a family. Your auto insurance policy, as well as other insurance policies, is something that definitely needs to be reviewed each year in conjunction with changes in your personal circumstances.

S: Is auto insurance required in New Hampshire?

P: An excellent question. I will discuss New Hampshire and Massachusetts automobile insurance as requirements differ by state. With the majority of our students coming from these two states, they provide good examples of some of the differences. Other states will have differences, but you will have a good understanding of what is covered in a policy.

New Hampshire does not require auto insurance; however an owner of a vehicle must be able to demonstrate that they are able to provide sufficient funds to meet New Hampshire Motor Vehicle Responsibility Requirements in the event of an "at fault" accident.

S: What does that mean?

P: Funny you should ask because, always having had insurance, I never understood the Responsibility Requirements before. I have never been asked for proof of insurance and any financial data when registering a car Looking at the website for the New Hampshire Division of Motor Vehicles, I'll give you some examples of when proof of insurance is required, (NHDS, 2018). These include, but are not limited to, convictions for Driving While Intoxicated (DWI), underage DWI, leaving the scene of an accident and conduct after an accident. If you have a bad driving record, many companies will not want to insure you so you will be assigned to the high-risk pool. I'll explain that later.

S: I'll assume a high-risk pool is not good.

P: Good assumption

S: Let's go through the basics of auto insurance.

P: I'll show you an actual policy as it will help you to follow along.

In Section A, you have liability which includes bodily injury and property damage. In New Hampshire the minimum limits are 25/50/25. What this means is that for an accident in which you are at fault, insurance will cover bodily injury claims of $25,000 per person and up to $50,000 in total if two or more people are injured. That is the 25/50 portion above. The 25 at the end means you are covered for up to $25,000 in property damage.

Amica Mutual Insurance Company
Concord Regional Office
5 Chenell Drive
Concord, NH 03301-8540
1-877-512-6422
1-877-512-6422

AUTO   HOME   LIFE

STATEMENT OF SAVINGS

Name and Address:
MICHAEL J. MC GUINNESS AND
MARY A. MC GUINNESS

Policy Number:

Your household's good driving history is reducing the price of your insurance! In addition to this good driving reward, you are receiving the following discounts and savings...

ANTI-THEFT DISCOUNT
MULTI-CAR DISCOUNT
PASSIVE RESTRAINT DISCOUNT
ELECTRONIC STABILITY CONTROL DISCOUNT
SIDE RESTRAINT DISCOUNT
LOYALTY DISCOUNT
CLAIM FREE DISCOUNT
MULTI-LINE DISCOUNT - HOME, PUP AND LIFE

TOTAL SAVINGS $

And still more savings...your estimated dividend!

As a policyholder you are eligible to receive declared dividends. The displayed estimate is based upon the latest dividend rate of **20** %. It reflects the amount that would be paid to you at the expiration of your policy using current information. Your actual dividend will be calculated using the rate declared by our Board of Directors and the rate in effect at time of your policy expiration. While a dividend is not guaranteed, Amica has paid dividends to policyholders every year since the company was founded in 1907. We are proud of this record and will continue to return as high a dividend as practical, consistent with sound business practices.

ESTIMATED DIVIDEND $

Call us 24 hours a day, seven days a week, to discuss your savings at 1-877-512-6422

CONTINUATION OF DECLARATIONS FOR PERSONAL AUTO POLICY NO.

NAMED INSURED
MICHAEL J. MC GUINNESS AND
MARY A. MC GUINNESS

COVERAGES	LIMIT OF LIABILITY		PREMIUMS	
COVERAGE IS PROVIDED WHERE A PREMIUM AND A LIMIT OF LIABILITY IS SHOWN FOR THE COVERAGE				
			AUTO 1 2007 TOYO	AUTO 2 2011 TOYO
A. LIABILITY	$ 250,000 each person		$	$
Bodily Injury	$ 500,000 each accident			
Property Damage	$ 50,000 each accident		$	$
B. MEDICAL PAYMENTS	$ 5,000 each person		$	$
C. UNINSURED MOTORISTS	$ 250,000 each person		$	$
Bodily Injury	$ 500,000 each accident			
D. DAMAGE TO YOUR AUTO (ACV means Actual Cash Value)				
1. Collision Loss	AUTO 1 AUTO 2			
ACV minus deductible of	$ 500 $ 500		$	$
2. Other Than Collision Loss	AUTO 1 AUTO 2			
ACV minus deductible of	$ 200 $ 200		$	$
TOWING AND LABOR COSTS $	each disablement			
OPTIONAL TRANSPORTATION EXPENSES				
AUTO 1 AUTO 2				

GARAGING LOCATION
1-OFF STREET
2-OFF STREET

TOTAL PREMIUM FOR EACH AUTO $ $

TOTAL PREMIUM $

CONTINUATION OF DECLARATIONS FOR PERSONAL AUTO POLICY NO.

NAMED INSURED
MICHAEL J. MC GUINNESS AND
MARY A. MC GUINNESS

SPECIAL DISCOUNTS

PASSIVE RESTRAINT DISCOUNT AUTO 1
ANTI-THEFT DEVICE DISCOUNT AUTOS 1,2
MULTI-LINE DISCOUNT-HOME, PUP AND LIFE
ELEC STABILITY CONTROL DISCOUNT AUTO 2
SIDE RESTRAINT DISCOUNT AUTO 2
CLAIM FREE DISCOUNT
MULTI-CAR DISCOUNT
LOYALTY DISCOUNT

Form and Endorsements made part of this policy at time of issue:

PP 00 01 01 05   PERSONAL AUTO POLICY
PP 13 06 01 09   CUSTOM EQUIPMENT EXCLUSION ENDORSEMENT
PP 01 76 02 17   AMENDMENT OF POLICY PROVISIONS - NEW HAMPSHIRE
AM 05 28 07 13   AMENDMENT OF PERSONAL AUTO POLICY PROVISIONS
PP 13 01 12 99   COVERAGE FOR DAMAGE TO YOUR AUTO EXCLUSION ENDORSEMENT
NH 04 45 10 17   UNINSURED MOTORISTS COVERAGE - NEW HAMPSHIRE
PP 23 40 10 15   PUBLIC OR LIVERY CONVEYANCE EXCLUSION ENDORSEMENT

This policy shall not be valid unless countersigned by our authorized agent or representative.

Countersigned by..... *Peter H. Cameron* .....

Authorized Representative

DECLARATIONS

PERSONAL AUTO POLICY NO.

NAMED INSURED AND ADDRESS
MICHAEL J. MC GUINNESS AND
MARY A. MC GUINNESS

POLICY PERIOD: 12:01 A.M., STANDARD TIME
From: NOVEMBER 15, 2017
To: NOVEMBER 15, 2018

Auto No.	DESCRIPTION OF AUTO(S) OR TRAILER(S)	LOSS PAYEE
1	2007 TOYOTA COROLLA CE/S/LE SEDAN VIN USE: AVERAGE DAILY MILEAGE MILES	
2	2011 TOYOTA CAMRY BASE/LE/SE/XLE SEDAN 4D VIN USE: AVERAGE DAILY MILEAGE MILES	

The Auto(s) or Trailer(s) described in this policy is principally garaged at the above address unless otherwise stated on the coverage pages.

SAFE DRIVER RATES APPLY.
RATES ARE BASED ON THE FOLLOWING HOUSEHOLD DRIVERS

Driver	NAME	DRIVER'S LICENSE NUMBER	Date of Birth Mo. Day Year	Male or Female	Married or Single	Date First Licensed Mo. Year
1	MICHAEL J. MC GUINNESS			M	M	
2	MARY A. MC GUINNESS			F	M	
3						
4						
5						
6						

S: I am not sure I understand. Can you give me an illustration?

P: Sure, you run a stop sign and hit a car injuring three people, and then crash into a building causing property damage. I'll call the three people A, B, and C. A has bodily injury claims of $30,000 against you, B had $20,000, and C has $15,000. The building has sustained $30,000 in damages.

Your insurance policy will pay $50,000 of the $65,000 in bodily injury claims. Only a maximum of $25,000 can be paid to A. If $25,000 is paid towards A, then only $25,000 of the potential $35,000 will be paid towards B and C. You will be paying $15,000 out of pocket for the balance.

With respect to the building, your policy will cover $25,000 of the $30,000, so you are paying $5,000 out of pocket.

I hate to give you further bad news, but the accident will drive up future insurance premiums.

S: Why does the policy you are showing me have 250,000/ 500,000/50,000 for these amounts?

P: Because, at this time, I have more assets than you so I have a lot more at risk. Remember that I mentioned, as your circumstances change, you want to relook at policies to make sure you are adequately covered.

S: Okay, I am following.

P: I'll give you one other fact for your memory bank. You'll be surprised how relatively small the additional cost is for incremental coverage, which is why you always ask for quotes when considering it. The cost of going from 25/50/25 to 250/500/50 coverage for a good driver is far less than you would think.

S: What about medical payments?

P: In New Hampshire, if you buy auto insurance for personal use, you must also buy at least $1,000 of medical payments coverage. It is really there for nuisance claims and hopefully you have adequate medical insurance to cover any injuries to you. It will cover you or anyone else in your car. It also covers you if you are struck while a pedestrian. Obviously bills will run far higher which is where other policies will need to come into play.

S: Uninsured motorists payments?

P: This provides coverage for damages to you or anyone in your vehicle in an accident involving an automobile driven by an individual who is uninsured or underinsured and who is found to be liable for your damages. As you can see in the policy we are looking at, similar to the liability section, the policy holder is covered for up to $250,000 for each person with a $500,000 maximum per accident.

You want to have underinsured motorists coverage, and please note that none of what we have discussed so far covers any damage to your car, which is where Section D comes into play.

S: I think I am starting to understand this policy. What is the difference between Sections 1 and 2 in Part D, what is ACV, and what is the deductible?

P: Let's talk Part 1 Collision Loss first. This is when your car has been damaged in an accident. The payment will be based on the actual cash value of the damages as determined by an insurance adjuster (the individual from the insurance company who assesses the damage to your car). Say your vehicle sustains $3,000 in damages, this policy holder would be reimbursed $2,500, which is the $3,000 less the $500 deductible. So the deductible is effectively what you are paying out of pocket for the accident.

S: But I didn't cause the accident so I don't want to pay the deductible.

P: Good point, if the other driver has been found to be at fault and your insurance company recovers the $3,000 from the other driver's insurance company, you will be reimbursed for the deductible.

But let's say that you were found to be at fault, in that case you will only be reimbursed the $2,500.

S: I still don't like the idea of this $500 deductible. What if I want a $0 deductible as I never want to have to pay out of pocket for damage to my car?

P: You can have your $0 deductible, but your policy cost will be higher. All insurance is about weighing trade-offs and figuring out what combination works best for you.

S: What is "other than collision?"

P: "Other than collision" covers damage to your automobile for many factors other than an accident. It will cover hail, water, vandalism, glass breakage, fire, and other assorted other factors. Note that the deductible is $200 here.

S: Towing and labor costs?

P: If your car breaks down and you need to get roadside assistance.

S: Why don't you have it?

P: I have AAA coverage. I strongly recommend this or another roadside program to anyone driving a car as I have found it invaluable and very cheap relative to the benefits provided.

S: And lastly, optional transportation expenses?

P: This will partly reimburse you for the cost of a rental car while your car is in the shop or while you are getting a new car. It covers a maximum amount per day and a maximum number of days.

S: I understand the basic policy provisions. How much is auto insurance going to cost me?

P: I wish the answer were that easy. As I mentioned, there are numerous factors in every type of insurance coverage. I will discuss these factors with you and then when buying insurance, I strongly recommend you get quotes from at least two companies on the exact same coverage.

S: How do I pick the insurance company? Let me guess, word of mouth?

P: Glad to see you have been listening and I will also reference Consumer Reports again here as they usually provide good rankings of many different aspects of insurance companies. An insurance agent is also good at shopping companies for you and acting on your behalf when claims arise.

S: You seem to put a lot of faith in Consumer Reports.

P: They have not steered me wrong yet.

S: Bad pun. So what are the factors?

P: I will give you many but I guarantee they are not all inclusive.

- Where the car will be located and driven
- The age of the driver
- The make, model, and cost of the car
- The driving history of the driver
- The coverage desired
- The deductibles chosen
- Where the car will be parked
- The mileage the car will be driven each year
- The credit history of the driver (although this is not applicable in Massachusetts and a few other states)
- The grades of the driver

S: Glad you did not give me the all-inclusive list. Let's go through some of these. Why does it matter where the car will be located and driven?

P: Think it through logically. Without saying a city or town is good or bad, do you think the chances of an automobile being stolen or in an accident are greater in Boston or Marblehead? Insurers determine rating territories and your car will fall into a rating territory.

S: What about age and sex?

P: Sad to say, the statistically proven worst drivers are males under 25. Males under 25 will pay more than females under 25 when all other factors are equal.

S: That's sex discrimination

P: Feel free to bring a case. Those are the facts.

S: I don't like it. I can understand a higher priced car costing more to insure than a lower cost car since the same accident would result in the insurance company paying out more. What about the driving history?

P: The worse your driving history is, the more you will pay. Running red lights, speeding, being the at fault driver in an accident, running a stop sign will all lead to "points" in the insurance world and just like golf, the more "points" you have, the worse off you are.

S: After our policy review, I have to believe that the higher the coverage you want and the lower the deductible, you will pay more. What about where the car is parked? That one makes no sense to me.

P: You'll notice on the policy at the bottom where it says garaging location. In this policy the two covered cars have an off-street location, meaning they are in a driveway or garage and not parked on the street at night. The chances of a car getting hit while parked are far lower in a driveway or garage than in the street, thus the cost is lower.

S: Mileage driven each year, obviously the more miles that you drive, the greater the chance of an accident. Do you have to send them weekly reports?

P: No, this is on the honor system but always subject to review if the insurance company desires after an accident.

S: Credit history? What does my credit history have to do with my ability to drive a car?

P: As we discuss in the Adult GPA section, your credit history is generally a pretty good indicator of your responsibility level. The less responsible you are, the greater the insurance risk you are. That said, if factors outside of your control such as illness or unexpected job loss are responsible for a poor credit history, discuss it with the insurance company and you may be given some leeway.

S: You are just giving me a hard time with the last one, grades, right?

P: I will certainly use every tool in the toolbox to get you to study more, but most insurance companies will reduce the insurance premiums of a student driver by $250 if he/she makes honor roll (high school) or dean's list (college). Hopefully, you'll get there; if you don't and your parents pay a significant part of your college costs and pay for your insurance coverage, I have full confidence you'll be giving them $250.

S: Enough there, any other factors?

P: Plenty but I'll just give you a few: any sort of anti-theft device is helpful; two or more cars leads to a multi-car discount; the more safety features in the car the better you are; having the policy for a number of years with the same insurer leads to discounts; no claims for a four-year period (in most cases); and I am sure you have seen a few of those Progressive commercials...what are Flo and her partner always preaching?

S: Wow, I am scared to tell you I remember this. Bundle...but what does that mean?

P: It means that if you have other lines of coverage with them such as homeowners, life, et cetera, you are paying less than if you just had an auto policy with them.

S: Information overload again in this section, but you have to have good auto insurance stories?

P: Too many unfortunately, but only one of them, I am glad to say, was my fault. I'll give you two of them as I learned things about my policy I did not know with these two illustrations.

In the first one, I hit a deer on a cold, rainy night. Nothing I could do. It was jumping from one side of 101 to the other and I did not see it until it was right in front of me. I drew the bad luck there as it easily could have been the car next to, in front of, or behind me. When I called the insurance company the next day and went through the details, I told them I knew I had the $500 deductible. They advised me that a deer falls under the "Other than Collision" category so I only had a $200 deductible.

With the second one, a car I had for three weeks was totaled from behind by a 22-year-old guy texting (what a coincidence, he fell into the worst ranked under 25 male category we were discussing). Again, I was looking at ACV minus the deductible and remember a car generally depreciates by $2,000 as soon as it is driven off the lot. I was pleasantly surprised when the insurance company told me that because I had the car less than 30 days, I would be reimbursed for what I paid for the car.

The key point is that the great majority of insurance companies play more than fair. When I hear of insurance headaches, I am immediately thinking "you picked the wrong insurer."

S: Hey Prof, I can't help but notice that you might need a new car.

P: Don't worry about me. The 2007 gets me where I want to go, and my wife drives the "new" one, the 2011.

S: But isn't the 2007 almost ready to go to the scrap heap?

P: Not at all. I did the proper due diligence and got myself a good car that I hope I can drive for at least another three years. Do you remember when we talked about leasing a car and discussed many leases being three years?

S: I do remember that.

P: Well, effectively I am well into my fourth three-year car lease, and haven't had a monthly payment in eight years. Any idea what my preference is?

S: Point taken. I hope I can get a car to last that long. On another subject, what is the dividend that is referenced?

P: There are two basic types of insurance companies, stock companies, and mutual companies. John Hancock is a stock company meaning there are stockholders. Any dividends are paid to a stockholder and policy holders are not necessarily stockholders.

Mutual companies are owned by those having insurance with the company. The dividend that you see is paid at the end of the policy year and has consistently been 20 percent of the cost of the policy. Amica, which is my insurer, and has written the policy that you see, is a mutual company.

S: Another thing to factor in when comparing companies?

P: Absolutely.

S: I hate to prolong this, but being from Massachusetts, can you tell me what the requirements for insurance in Massachusetts are?

P: Easily done. In Massachusetts you are required to have four different types of car insurance with the following minimums: ("Car Insurance," n.d.)

1. Bodily Injury to Others
   $20,000 per person
   $40,000 per accident

2. Personal Injury Protection
   $8,000 per person in an accident

3. Bodily Injury Caused by an Uninsured Auto
   $20,000 per person
   $40,000 per accident

4. Damage to Someone Else's Property
   $5,000 per accident

S: Not a lot of coverage, is it?

P: I am not evaluating your driving ability, but as you begin to accumulate assets, you'd better have far more! One other thing about Massachusetts is that your credit history cannot enter into the policy cost calculation.

S: Also, you mentioned earlier about a high-risk pool. I'm guessing we are not talking about a swimming pool.

P: Thanks for reminding me. If you have an absolutely horrendous driving record, no company wants to insure you, but the state wants you insured.

S: So what happens?

P: In exchange for being allowed to offer insurance in the state, each insurer must participate in the high-risk pool whereby they must insure drivers assigned by the state. Think of it as losing the lottery.

S: Great, so I'll get the same price as their customers?

P: Sure you will, after the price is adjusted for your horrendous driving record.

S: I get the point, it will be expensive.

P: Yes, time to reduce spending for other accounts in your budget.

RENTING AN APARTMENT

STUDENT: I can't wait to get my own apartment when I get out of school. Can we talk about what I should consider when looking for an apartment?

PROFESSOR: Many things to consider here but first, I'll tell you to consider living with your parents for a year or two if it is feasible for them and for your work location. While it may cramp your social lifestyle, you can save a significant amount of money for a year or two. In fact, if your parents are letting you live for free, work out an arrangement to pay them fair market rent each month and they can put it away into an account and give you the lump sum when you ultimately depart.

This approach will strengthen your budgeting skills as you will be dealing with a significant fixed cost each month. You will quickly learn to allocate the rest of your take-home pay.

S: I'll consider that, but let's look at the rental process.

P: Will do, let's just take a look at some of the key general questions before considering questions specific to a unit:

- Where do you want to live?
- In those towns you are considering, what specific section of the town are you looking at?
- What are the average rental rates in the areas you are looking at?
- Do you want to live in a complex or in a family duplex; two or three-decker?
- What do you want for amenities?
- Will you have roommates and how many?
- Would you consider becoming a roommate of someone already renting an apartment?

S: That's a lot of questions right off the start.

P: They certainly are but these will come to you naturally as you start thinking things through.

S: Okay, let's start to look at questions specific to a unit.

P: First and foremost is how much can you afford? Generally, experts say no more than 25 percent to 30 percent of your gross income should be spent on rent itself (not considering the other costs of an apartment). I have taken the liberty of pulling the information regarding an opinion from one realtor from the Quicken.com website.

"According to CBS MoneyWatch, some landlords require that you spend no more than a quarter of your pre-tax income on rent—rent being the operative word. Forget utilities and other associated expenses for the moment. 'Rent generally should not be more than 25 percent of your gross monthly salary,' says Andy Solari, realtor associate at Re/Max Carrier Realtors in Brigantine, New Jersey.

'If an individual's income is \$4,000 a month, then the rent should be no higher than \$1,000." ("How Much Should," n.d.)

S: People say too much information is dangerous and I am starting to believe that. When we talked about taxes, you said that I would be paying 7.65 percent for Social Security and Medicare, a marginal federal rate of probably 12 percent, a marginal state rate of maybe 4 percent (depending on what state I am living and working in). So, if I am running these numbers in my head correctly, with 25 percent going to rent, about 50 percent of my monthly income is already spent. Living with my parents is starting to look a little bit better.

P: Hopefully from their side also! The marginal impact is not equal throughout the year, but that discussion would only confuse the issue. Let's use the 50 percent at this time.

S: I am going to have to go back and review our discussion on budgeting. I was half listening at the time, but I am certainly seeing the importance now.

P: Thanks for your honesty. I am happy you were half listening. Now back to the specific rental questions:

- What are the other costs associated with the rental? Heat, water, electricity, parking, et cetera. Make sure whenever you are talking with a potential lessor (the person or company renting to you), you ask them for all other associated costs.
- How long a lease do you need to sign?
- Do you have the ability to allow others to live with you if you are originally starting out solo?

- How much is the security deposit? What other "up front" payments are necessary?
- Are pets allowed?

S: Irrelevant to me. I am not planning on having a pet.

P: May be quite relevant to you. If pets are allowed and your neighbor has a barking dog, you will quickly rue your rental decision. There is even a *Seinfeld* episode where Elaine is hiring Newman to "knock off" a neighbor's barking dog. Now back to the specific questions:

- Are you able to sublet the unit if circumstances change?
- Are there laundry facilities available?
- If a complex, is there a fitness center and does that require an additional fee?
- Do you get allocated one or two parking spaces if there is a lot for the complex?

If you are in a complex, make sure you understand all the amenities offered, all the related restrictions, and any relevant costs of using the amenities.

S: I never really gave it much thought as to living in a complex or living in a two or three decker or duplex. Any major differences?

P: There certainly are. If your lessor is living in the same building as you, you may be under constant scrutiny as to parties, guests, et cetera. The last thing they want to see is you hosting a party with 30 people present. However, more importantly, you may have the ability to negotiate the agreed rent with them.

S: Why with a single landlord and not a complex?

P: The complex is a much more formal arrangement and you are another potential lessee (the renting person) to them. If you don't take it, someone else eventually will. With the single landlord, believe it or not, you are a very desirable tenant as a young professional. The biggest headache for any landlord is "the tenant from hell" so, if they like you, they may be willing to cut you a break as you will bring far fewer headaches than other possibilities.

If a non-complex rental, what are the parking arrangements? What happens when there is significant snowfall?

S: Oh boy! I remember auto insurance costs will differ depending on off-street versus on-street parking. All these things we are discussing are interrelated, aren't they?

P: Absolutely, and there is much more to discuss.

S: Let's say I have done my—as you would call it—"due diligence" and am ready to rent. What else should I do?

P: Do a good visual inspection of the apartment: open and close windows, doors, check the flooring, run water, flush the toilet, turn on the shower, et cetera. Make sure everything, at least for now, is functioning as it should.

Now if you think you are ready, do a video-taping, ideally with the landlord present, of the premises. With that, you have documented the status of the apartment at the time of your rental. When your lease comes to an end, your landlord will do a walk-through and deduct any assessed damage from your security deposit. Hopefully, you will get it all back unlike living in a college dorm where some knucklehead(s) is (are) undoubtedly costing everyone else some portion of their security deposit.

You also want to know, prior to signing the lease, when your security deposit will be returned. In the old days, when interest rates were higher, you would earn interest on your security deposit. No need to ask any questions about interest at this time.

S: Anything else I should know?

P: You definitely want to have renters insurance.

S: Another cost?

P: This one is dirt cheap relative to the potential benefit if misfortune occurs. It will probably be $200 - $250 a year. It provides coverage against fire, vandalism and theft, and it also covers clothes, electronics, furnishings, and other belongings, even if they're elsewhere, such as in a car.

It will also cover liability protection against claims for bodily injury and extra expenses for hotel bills when an apartment becomes uninhabitable due to a covered loss.

We'll discuss Homeowner's Insurance at a later time which will give you a much broader look into insurance coverage because I am hoping you will be going from an apartment to a home if you manage your money wisely as we have discussed.

S: I hope so also.

P: One last bit of advice. When you are going to view a rental property, take a friend with you and make sure someone else knows where you and your friend are going and at what time.

S: You're kidding me with this one, right?

P: Unfortunately, no. You are going to meet someone you don't know at a location that you may not know. I would say 99.9 percent of the time it is not an issue, but I'll recommend the more cautious approach here.

S: Thanks, I'll keep that in mind.

HOME BUYING

STUDENT: I would love to own a home at some point. Can we go through what is involved in buying a home similar to what we did with buying a car?

PROFESSOR: We certainly can. Let's just figure out what you are looking for in terms of a home.

S: What do you mean here? A house is a house, right?

P: Based on your comments I am assuming you are talking about a single family home.

S: I guess I am, but what other types of properties are there and what are the differences?

P: Now you are asking the right questions. I'll briefly explain the most common forms of home ownership. Note that I am not talking about the way the property will be titled (i.e. in whose name(s)), but the type of property ownership you are buying.

The single family home is what you are probably most familiar with. With this generally, you own the home and the property and can do what you want with it as long as you are not violating any zoning laws.

S: What is a zoning law?

P: Please note that we will bounce around among topics as you ask questions, but ask away as you have them.

Zoning laws in a community dictate how property can be used. In the simplest explanation, if it is zoned residential, only dwelling units can be located there. If it is zoned commercial, a business can be located there, and if it is zoned mixed use, it can be either residential or commercial.

S: If I am buying a single family home, why do I need to worry about that?

P: Well if you have vacant lots close to you, you will want to know the zoning of those lots. I am guessing you are not going to want businesses located close to your home if they are bringing in excess volumes of traffic, not to mention the parking hassles of guests visiting you.

S: Good point, another thing to remember.

P: Lots to remember. A good realtor will help you with the process, but before we discuss the realtor's role, let's get back to housing types. Staying with the single family home, you will want to know if the house is part of a homeowners association.

S: Why is that?

P: Well, chances are the homeowners association will have rules that will restrict the use of your property and what can be on your property. In addition to that, you will have a monthly fee to pay so you will want to know that for sure.

S: How can they restrict the use of my property and what type of restrictions are they?

P: By buying property in this area, you are de facto joining the homeowers association. There will be bylaws which may say such things as no clotheslines on the property, no pools, no excess size flags, et cetera. You definitely want to see what restrictions are before buying the property.

S: What does the homeowners association do for me?

P: There may be a common recreational area with a pool, tennis courts, children play area, et cetera. They cover the maintenance, upkeep, and liability insurance with this common area property. Perhaps if it is a private development, they need to pay for snow-plowing and other services. The key is to know the restrictions, the cost, and I would also suggest knowing the financial situation of the homeowners association.

S: This is way too much. Why do I need to know the financial situation of the homeowners association?

P: You don't but I would suggest it. If they are in tough financial shape and need additional finances beyond the monthly fees, there will be a special assessment (i.e. additional one-time charge) to all homes within the association. Let's get back to the types of houses now.

There are multi-unit houses which could entail two or three story dwelling units, duplexes, and townhouses. Generally if you buy a two or three story dwelling unit or a duplex, you are buying the land and the property. With a townhouse, you are buying a unit and have common areas to be covered via a homeowners association or similar group.

S: So I buy a two or three story home or a duplex, I can rent out the unit(s) that I don't live in and generate revenue. Any downside here?

P: It generally works for people, but you need to be careful. If your tenants aren't paying their rent, you are chasing them down which is most likely time consuming and may be costly. If you get the "tenants from hell," it may be a long and painful process before you can get them evicted. It will be no fun living in the same building with them as this process occurs. Remember when we were talking about renting an apartment and I told you to try to negotiate the rent if possible because you were a desirable tenant? You are now on the other side of the equation looking for desirable tenants.

Also when you were renting and had a problem at 2:00 a.m., you would not hesitate to call a number to get some assistance. Guess who is getting that phone call at 2:00 a.m. now?

S: So I need to do my "due diligence?"

P: Now I am impressed. You probably know people who live in a condominium. Some of these were apartments before they became condominiums. With a condominium, you own a unit in a building, you have common ownership of the building and all the associated property.

S: There has to be some sort of a homeowners association then?

P: Very impressive again, it is generally a condo association and everything we discussed with respect to a homeowners association is applicable.

There is also a form of housing called cooperative ("co-op") housing. These generally exist in big cities and are very costly so I won't get into that now. There is a *Seinfeld* episode that partially covers co-op housing.

S: Why do you keep referring to *Seinfeld* episodes?

P: Sad to say, there are many situations in life that can be explained by reference to a *Seinfeld* episode despite its being a show about nothing.

S: How do I decide where I want to live? What are the most important factors?

P: The one real estate principle that most people agree on are that the three most important factors are "location, location, location."

S: So by location you mean city or town?

P: City or town and location within the city or town. You are looking for a city or town with a good school system and offers the most upside for appreciation in the value of your property.

S: But what if I don't plan on having a family and plan on living in the same house for 40 years? Why do I care about the school system and why should I pay for it if I am not going to have kids?

P: Good questions, but facts and circumstances change and no matter where you live, the cost of the school system will be a significant factor in your property taxes. Parents want a good school system for their children so it creates demand within that city, and demand drives property values.

If your facts and circumstances change and you need to sell your house, you want as much appreciation as possible when it comes time to sell. And remember, location within the city or town is important too as some schools within a city are known for being better than others.

S: Sounds like a lot more "due diligence."

P: Well worth the invested time. What you will learn is the more due diligence you do, the better you will become. There is a learning curve and much of your due diligence is applicable to different areas.

S: Okay, what is the realtor going to do for me?

P: First of all, you want to find a realtor…

S: Sorry to interrupt, but word of mouth right?

P: Not a bad way, hopefully you have some friends or associates who have had a good experience with a realtor and that is a good starting point.

S: What is the realtor going to do for me, and how much will it cost me?

P: Your realtor will be known as the buyer's realtor and it will cost you nothing.

S: This makes no sense, why is this realtor going to work for me for free?

P: Because they will receive a portion of the commission on the sale of the house and it is generally paid by the seller.

S: You mean I might have to pay it.

P: Only if the seller convinces you to through negotiation, so hopefully you won't be agreeing to this unless there is a very unusual set of facts and circumstances.

S: So what will my realtor get paid, and what will my realtor do for me?

P: The normal real estate commission is 6 percent so if you are buying a $300,000 home, your realtor will get $4,500 and your realtor's agency will get $4,500. Likewise, the seller's realtor will get $4,500 and his/her agency will get $4,500. We'll go through a mortgage closing statement at a later time so you can visualize the transaction.

You will want to lay out parameters for your realtor in terms of:

- Where you would like to live
- What type of house you are looking for
- What type of neighborhood you are looking for
- Any other items of specific relevance to you
- Approximately how much you are looking to pay for a house

Your realtor will know if what you are willing to pay is feasible for where you would like to live, and will know current availability and units as they come to market.

He/she will schedule with you to take you to see homes in which you might be interested. You may also find something of interest on your own. If you find your realtor is taking you to many properties which are not in line with your parameters, you are probably better off finding another realtor.

S: What happens when I have found something in which I am interested?

P: Your realtor should help you in developing a bid for the home which he/she will ultimately present to the seller's agent. The seller may not accept your offer, in which case the seller can give you a counteroffer and you can deliver another offer. Your realtor will work with you through this process.

S: Assuming my bid or the counteroffer is accepted, then what happens?

P: A purchase and sale (P&S) agreement will be created. You may be asked to put down a deposit which will be held in escrow, which I will discuss further with you. Your offer will be contingent on getting financing (which hopefully you have lined up in advance), a satisfactory home inspection, and an appraisal of the property by your lender.

Your realtor will work with you throughout the process right up until the actual closing, so no commissions are due until the deal is done.

S: How much of a deposit do I have to put down?

P: It can vary, so I hate to give you a number here as it may be a wide range.

S: What if I decide I don't want the house after signing the purchase and sale agreement?

P: If it is because you changed your mind, and not because of an unsatisfactory home inspection or your being unable to obtain financing, you will most likely lose your deposit.

S: I guess I better be sure. How much does a home inspection and an appraisal cost?

P: A home inspection will probably cost you $300 - $500, but it is critical. You want to ensure all systems are tested, the furnace examined, any appliances to be included, electrical, roofing, if you have a well and septic system. In short, any item that would take significant dollars to be repaired needs to be tested.

S: I get to keep the appliances.

P: You will negotiate that as part of your offer. If there is anything within the house that you want to keep, it can be negotiated with the seller. Rely on your realtor's expertise here.

S: Sounds fair. What about if I want to use the seller's realtor also?

P: Not a good idea, there is a potential for a conflict of interest if the same realtor represents the buyer and seller. If it turns out that your realtor is showing you many homes for which his/her agency is the selling realtor, you will want to again consider changing realtors. Not to say there have not been deals done this way, but I would shy away from it.

S: I have a good basic understanding. What about getting the mortgage now and figuring out my monthly payments?

P: Excellent point. Mortgages are a separate topic of discussion. I will get into mortgage loans and other types of loans with you as one topic.

THE MORTGAGE PROCESS

PROFESSOR: Well, let's go slowly with this one. Before you even have a purchase agreement on a house, I would suggest that you get pre-approved for a mortgage. In that way, you should minimize surprises. If you know how much you are approved for, you know what you can afford to bid for a house assuming you have a good estimate of insurance and property tax costs.

S: You mean I can get pre-approved for a mortgage?

P: You certainly can.

S: So where do I go?

P: You have plenty of choices here. You can easily review mortgage rates of many banks and credit unions on their websites. That will give you an idea of the bank or credit union with which you may want to deal. There are mortgage brokers who will shop for the best rate for you, but remember they are getting a fee. I would not recommend them for your first house. I would work with a small local bank or credit union as, in my opinion, they will give you the "hands on" direction that you will most likely need.

S: Word of mouth here?

P: Will generally be good. Most people are happy to tell you if they had a good or bad experience with the mortgage process.

S: What will I need to get pre-approved?

P: There are three key things with respect to your mortgage application, namely income, assets, and credit but I am guessing you will be in better shape than you think.

If you have been working for two years, most lending institutions will want two years of your W-2s (the end of year statements showing your earnings for the year). Recent college graduates do not need a two-year employment history; in some instances the offer letter and recent paystubs are sufficient.

S: What if I have been self-employed, which I am hoping I can do?

P: If you are self-employed, they will want your last two years of tax returns.

S: What about if I worked and also had a second job?

P: They will want to see two years of the W-2 related to the second job also. They want to ensure any second job will provide a steady source of additional income if it is to be used in evaluating your loan.

S: What if I worked under the table?

P: Well, first of all, you, most likely, owe additional federal income taxes, but let's take that off the table. If it is a second job, the proof is a W-2.

S: I'll get the employer for my second job to prepare a letter and have it notarized.

P: No good. No W-2 means no additional income for a mortgage loan.

They will review your credit report, including your FICO score. Let's assume for the moment that you have heeded the advice of many over the years and have a good credit score, so that is not an issue. Your credit report shows required monthly payments such as car loans or student loans. You know enough to pay off your credit card balances each month, but even if you have a significant credit card balance, the amount used is the minimum required balance due, which is usually low since the credit card companies love the interest.

S: Information overload again, Prof. Give me some numbers.

P: Understood. Many credit cards have a minimum payment due of 2 percent of the outstanding balance, so if you have $5,000 outstanding—which I hope you don't—the amount used in the mortgage analysis will be $100.

S: So what is the magic number that comes out of all this?

P: It will be, can your required monthly debt payments in total be within 33–43 percent of your monthly gross income? In certain circumstances they can go a bit higher than 43 percent, but let's use that as the upper limit now. Let's assume some monthly debt payments.

S: I'll assume $300 per month for a car payment and $250 per month on my student loans.

P: And how much income do you want to assume?

S: Let's say $70,000 per year. Are we going to run through a mathematical exercise again?

P: You know it. And you can do it, you've shown you are above average in quickly figuring out the math. Let's see you do it again.

S: Well if I am making $70,000 per year, my gross is $5,833 per month. I have $550 in required monthly payments. 43 percent of my gross is $2,508 so I can afford a mortgage that is $1,958 per month.

P: Nice calculation. While the mortgage covers principal and interest, you have at least three other required payments now occurring, namely property taxes, homeowners insurance, and mortgage insurance. If you are buying a condo, you also have your monthly condo fee. Likewise, if you are buying a house with a homeowners association, you have that monthly payment.

S: Thanks for the extra information. I know the dollar value of the house I can afford just went down.

P: Unless you have a person willing to give you a gift for a big down payment.

S: Big picture now, how much house can I afford and how do I know the cost of all the other items you just laid on me?

P: Those are easily estimated. We need to look at mortgage rates and then we can start to ballpark how much house you can afford. But first let's cover some other items with respect to the mortgage process.

S: What is out there for mortgage programs?

P: There are conventional mortgages where you go to a bank or credit union and you will have a higher down payment than some of the special programs. So there will be some significant dollars involved between the down payment and closing costs.

S: My parents said they will try to help me out with the down payment. Will that reduce the amount of money I can potentially borrow?

P: Not at all but…they must sign a letter clearly stating that the money does not have to be repaid.

S: I was planning on repaying them.

P: That is something you need to work out with your parents. The rule is clear though with respect to the letter.

S: Any tax consequences?

P: Tax course! Your parents can give you up to $28,000 per year without having to file a gift tax return. They can also do the same for your spouse or significant other also.

S: They are going to owe taxes if they give me more than $28,000?

P: No, they just need to file a return and for the great majority of people, there will be no tax consequences during life or at the time of death.

S: What are some of the non-conventional mortgages?

P: If you are not making a lot of money and want to live in a town with less than 35,000 people, the U.S. Department of Agriculture has a loan program to help you out.

If you are a veteran with an honorable discharge, you can get a loan with no down payment. There is a funding fee of 3 percent, which is added to the loan amount.

The Federal Housing Administration will give you a mortgage with a 3.5 percent down payment for a credit score of at least 580. If you are lower than 580, a 10 percent down payment will be required.

S: 580?? And after all you told me about the importance of credit scores?

P: If your credit score is that low, it means you have significant financial issues with which to deal and most banks/lenders that offer FHA will not go that low. It will definitely cost you in other areas so you need to keep your credit score high.

I am just mentioning these other possibilities but I strongly recommend, as I already mentioned, going to a small local bank or credit union and working with them as they will give you the necessary guidance

S: One last question in this area. You said the FHA will definitely cost you in other areas. What do you mean by that?

P: You'll need to carry private mortgage insurance (PMI) over the life of the loan.

S: What is PMI?

P: PMI protects the lender in case of a default. It covers the lender for its loss after it forecloses on and sells a home.

S: What is the cost of PMI?

P: It varies but it can range from 0.5 percent to 1 percent of the outstanding mortgage balance.

S: I know, let's look at the math.

P: Sure thing, let's go with a $200,000 mortgage and we'll use 0.75 percent. Your cost will be $125 per month

S: I must be able to get rid of this at some point.

P: With an FHA loan that is incorrect. It is required over the life of the loan.

S: What about with a conventional loan?

P: With a conventional loan and a 20 percent down payment, you can request that you not pay PMI. If you put less than 20 percent down, when you get to having paid 20 percent of the original loan balance, you can cancel it via a formal request process. When you get to having paid 22 percent of the original loan balance, it is automatically cancelled.

S: So if I understand you correctly, with an FHA loan, I always have this $125 monthly payment and if I put 20 percent down with a conventional loan, I save this $125?

P: Financial alternatives once again!

S: Any tax consequences with PMI?

P: There was through 2017, but no longer. You know my answer to that.

S: I know, tax course! But the changes have made the tax law much easier.

P: To many taxpayers, but I still recommend taking the course. As I have said, knowing the tax consequences before making a decision can prove beneficial.

S: Choices, choices, less than 20 percent down payment with a FHA loan but the extra $125 per month. Conventional loan with 20 percent down, save $125 per month. Anything else with a conventional mortgage?

P: Well, that all-important FICO score is going to come into play again. Different banks have different FICO requirements for a conventional mortgage. You want as high a FICO score as possible.

S: Why can't there be just one set of rules?

P: Options, options, options. You can always better your situation with options. That is not true with one set of rules so always know your options.

S: My parents would like me to have a house even if I don't have a job. Is this possible?

P: Your parents are much nicer than I am. Even if you have no credit, your parents can co-sign a loan for you. With all due respect to you and your parents, I would not recommend that. However, if you have bad credit, you can't get a mortgage even if your parents are willing to co-sign the loan.

S: Okay, time to start making some money and starting to figure out my options. We have talked about the process and potential sources for the mortgage, but earlier in the discussion we started talking about some hypothetical numbers and how much of a mortgage I can afford. Can we go back to that?

P: Most certainly.

MORTGAGE OPTIONS

STUDENT: I am ready to see theoretically how much house I can afford. Yet another mathematical exercise.

PROFESSOR: I'll warn you, you haven't liked having to evaluate financial alternatives so you won't like this topic much at all. To add insult to injury, I am even going to cover a possibility which is not even demonstrated on the schedules we will be looking at.

S: Oh joy, I can hardly wait.

P: First, we'll look at adjustable rate mortgages (ARM) but, at this time, I would only consider an ARM under special circumstances.

S: Why and what?

P: We'll get to that in due course.

First, with the ARMs, you will notice four types.

S: I notice that. I see 1 Year, 3/1 Year, 5/1 Year, 10/1 Year. I also notice that as you go out in time...I am assuming that is what the numbers following one year are doing, the rates increase. Now, when we talked about savings, we saw that the longer you were willing to tie up your money, the higher the rate the bank would pay.

The index for all of the below ARM programs equals one year U.S. Constant Maturity

ADJUSTABLE RATE MORTGAGES						
TYPE	**RATE**	**POINTS**	**APR**	**CAPS**	**MARGIN**	**MONTHLY PAYMENT PER $1,000**
1 Year ARM	2.625%	0.000%	4.398%	2/6%	3.000%	$4.02
3/1 Year ARM	2.875%	0.000%	4.179%	2/6%	3.000%	$4.15
5/1 Year ARM	3.125%	0.000%	4.059%	2/6%	3.000%	$4.28
10/1 Year ARM	3.625%	0.000%	4.010%	2/6%	3.000%	$4.56

P: Excellent. Now what do you think is happening here?

S: Well, you are now taking out the loan and I am guessing the longer they are extending money to you, the higher the rate they want.

P: Excellent again! That is exactly what is happening. They are now absorbing the risk of higher interest rates with future inflation possible so they want more to cover their risk.

S: What does the /1 mean?

P: With an ARM, the /1 means that the rate will be adjusted every year at the same date after the initial period you have chosen.

S: So if I take a 3/1, it will adjust after the third year, a 5/1 after the fifth year and a 10/1 after the 10th year?

P: Spot on!

S: Well what about the 1 Year ARM?

P: The rate adjusts after one year.

S: I'm not sure I like this. They can adjust the rate to any rate they want?

P: Not at all. Like any good business deal, all the key parameters are clearly defined.

S: And why don't I see this at this time?

P: Because I haven't explained how to read the information to you yet.

S: Okay, let's go.

P: The key is how the rates can change after the initial period and each subsequent year after that. Read me the line just above the Adjustable Rate Mortgages table.

S: "The index for all of the below ARM programs equals one year U.S. Treasury Constant Maturity." What the heck does that mean?

P: That is the benchmark by which your rate will be reset at each reset period.

S: I'm still lost. Where do I find such a rate?

P: Easy search. I just saw the rate on the Saint Louis Fed (one of the 12 Federal Reserve Banks) and, as of today (November 8, 2017) it is 1.53 percent. (FRB of St. Louis, n.d.)

S: Wow, so if I take a 1 Year ARM at 2.625 percent, and this rate does not change, my rate will adjust to 1.53 percent? Sign me up.

P: If only it were that nice. Unfortunately, the banks will be in more trouble than when they sank themselves in 2008 and 2009.

Can you find a column called Margin?

S: Yes, I see it. Three percent for all the ARMs...what does this do?

P: That is what will be added to the one year U.S. Treasury Constant Maturity rate.

S: Wait...so you are saying if that rate does not change in the next year and I took the 1 Year ARM, that my rate will change to 4.53 percent?

P: Now you understand it.

S: But what would that do to my mortgage payment?

P: Well, fortunately I have a handy Excel spreadsheet where we can run computations for all sets of numbers. It shows how a mortgage is amortized (paid off) showing the breakdown between principal and interest for each payment. Remember when we talked about amortization when discussing car loans?

S: I do and I assume principal payments reduce my balance?

P: That is correct. I'll give you some monthly intervals of the first 60 months of an amortization schedule later so let's look at some hypotheticals now. How much do you want to assume for a mortgage?

S: Let's say $200,000 and now that you have my undivided attention, can you do it for all four mortgage possibilities?

P: Sure can, you are learning quickly and I will assume that the 1 Year Constant Maturity Rate stays at 1.53 percent but, in my opinion, this is a wildly optimistic assumption. It is going up, but we want to look at things consistently.

S: I don't think I am going to like any of the answers.

P: Nor do I, but here we go…if you had taken a 1 Year ARM, your monthly principal and interest (P&I) would be $804. At the end of the first year, your mortgage balance would be $195,459 and your monthly P&I payment would increase to $1,010.

S: That's crazy.

P: Just one of the alternatives you are investigating. We'll run the other combinations now.

3/1 ARM	Initial P&I $830	Balance at end of 3 years $186,826	New P&I $1,000
5/1 ARM	Initial P&I $856	Balance at end of 5 years $178,264	New P&I $994
10/1 ARM	Initial P&I $912	Balance at end of 10 years $155,557	New P&I $987

S: With all due respect Professor, I think you've lost a little off your fastball. Those numbers have to be in error because they make no sense at all. Basically you are telling me that with a 10/1 ARM, I have made total P&I payments at the end of 10 years of $109,440 ($912 * 120 months), yet I have only paid off $44,443 of my principal ($200,000 - $155,557). And, on top of that, my P&I payment goes up by $75? Might be time to consider leaving academia and spending more time on the course.

P: I always liked your bluntness, but I don't want to beat you more badly on the course than I already do. Those numbers reflect the reality of the situation which is why you choose your alternative carefully. O ye, of little faith, as I said, we will look at parts of an amortization schedule and you will see the reality of the situation.

S: All right, I will trust you for now. I don't need the embarrassment of getting additional strokes from you.

Now I understand the APR based on prior discussions, what is the column labeled "Caps?"

P: Good question. The two says that the most your interest rate can go up in any reset period is 2 percent while the most the rate can go up over the life of the loan is 6 percent. To illustrate using the 1/1 ARM, if the 1 Year Treasury Constant Maturity Rate at the end of the first year is 2.1 percent, then mathematically your rate resets to 5.1 percent (2.1% + 3%). However, due to the Cap, it can only reset to 4.625 percent (2.625% + 2%). Either way, the outcome is not pleasant, and you are already well on your way to an increase at the end of the second year.

S: Could the 1 Year Constant Maturity Rate increase that much in a year?

P: I'll answer that question by telling you that a year ago the rate was 0.71 percent.

S: So the highest my rate can go up to is 8.625 percent. Can we run numbers with that scenario?

P: Take my word for it. It would be ugly and the numbers would only depress you.

S: Well, the fixed rate option is looking better for me. I see the 30 year fixed rate mortgage is 4 percent and the monthly P&I payment would be approximately $955 (note: calculation per bank schedule is $954; actual payment would be $954.83). I could handle that.

OWNER OCCUPIED FIXED RATES — SERVICING RETAINED

TYPE	RATE	POINTS	APR	MONTHLY PAYMENT PER $1,000
30 Year Fixed	4.000%	0.000%	4.051%	$4.77
15 Year Fixed	3.500%	0.000%	3.590%	$7.15

Conventional mortgages 20% down with minimum FICO score of 740

NON-OWNER OCCUPIED MORTGAGES

TYPE	RATE	POINTS	CAPS	MARGIN
1 Year ARM	4.000%	0.000%	2/6%	3.500%
3/1 Year ARM	4.250%	0.000%	2/6%	3.500%
5/1 Year ARM	4.500%	0.000%	2/6%	3.500%

P: I am glad to see you are feeling comfortable with these tables.

S: The 15 year fixed rate mortgage carries a lower rate because a shorter loan period is less risk for the bank, so at 3.5 percent the payment on a 15 year mortgage would be about $1,430. Wow! I would have thought that would be a lot more. It is only $475 more to pay the mortgage off in half the time.

What would you recommend?

P: Again, this is personal preference. I have always preferred the 15 year mortgage, but would have no trouble with a 30 year mortgage. You need to make sure the extra $475, that a 15 year mortgage will cost you, is not causing you financial issues with another payment or your monthly expenses. Likewise, thinking ahead to investments, these are great rates if you think you could invest the $475 lower payment from a 30 year mortgage at more than 4 percent, the 30 year mortgage is a very viable alternative. But don't take any investment returns as guaranteed unless they are, and remember all the CD rates we saw were well below 4 percent.

S: Any lengths in between 15 years and 30 years?

P: Some banks have other options such as a 20 or 25 year mortgage. You now know that all you need to do is ask.

S: Any other suggestions?

P: If you go for the 30 year mortgage and the lower monthly payment, you can increase your payment in any given month and if you think about it, it is investing money at 4 percent. You need to understand that you cannot pull it back from the mortgage balance if you need it later; once it is in, it stays. However, just to give you an illustration, if you were to pay an extra $100 each month with the $955 payment, you would pay the mortgage off in 301 months or just over 25 years; with an extra $200 per month, it would be 259 months or just over 21 and a half years. It is the value of compound interest that we discussed so long ago.

S: I like these options. Now reading the rate sheets, I see that this is for a conventional mortgage with a 20 percent down payment and a 740 minimum FICO score. I see the FICO score has great importance for a conventional mortgage loan.

Why would the non-owner occupied rates be higher than owner occupied, and why are there no fixed rate offerings?

P: Think this one through yourself.

S: Well risk versus reward has been a constant throughout everything we discussed, so I am guessing there is more risk if the owner does not live on the property, therefore it comes at a higher rate.

P: You're ready to start explaining this and other areas.

S: What about the home equity lines?

HOME EQUITY LOANS (FIXED RATE)

LOAN AMOUNT	MAXIMUM LOAN TO VALUE	RATE	APR	TERM (UP TO) MONTHS	MONTHLY PAYMENT PER $10,000
Minimum loan amount is $10,000 and the maximum is $250,000	80% of Appraised Value	3.625%	3.682%	60	$182.48
Minimum loan amount is $10,000 and the maximum is $250,000	80% of Appraised Value	4.125%	4.155%	120	$101.84
Minimum loan amount is $10,000 and the maximum is $250,000	80% of Appraised Value	4.625%	4.646%	180	$77.14

P: Those allow you to borrow more once you have been in your house and built some equity. You should not be worrying about those until after you have been in your house for a while, so I will go through those with you sometime in the future. The principles are exactly the same though and I am fully confident you can understand them by reading the tables.

S: What do you mean by "built some equity"?

P: It means that you have been able to reduce your mortgage balance by a fairly good amount and your home has increased in value.

S: Got it! Now you said you would only consider an ARM under special circumstances. What would those be?

P: Firstly, I think interest rates are going up and going up significantly moving forward. Even if I hit my batting average of being wrong one-half of the time, the potential decreases from what interest rates are now are far less than the potential increases.

With that first thought in mind (that rates should be increasing), an ARM only makes sense if you are planning on selling your house before your first reset period kicks in. For example, if you think you will be moving in eight years, the 10 year ARM would make sense for you. Remember though that nothing is certain...

S: Except death and taxes!

P: You're ahead of me there, but it is difficult to see where you might be in eight years or how your facts and circumstances have changed. All I am saying is, proceed with caution.

S: What is the possibility you discussed not documented on the rate schedule?

P: That would be points, which you see are all 0.0 percent. Ask your parents about points as there are all sort of opinions about them. As interest rates rise (again, in my opinion), you will probably see points reappear in the future. Each point is 1 percent of the loan value so, for the hypothetical $200,000 mortgage we looked at, one point would be $2,000 and two points would be $4,000. When rates were high, you would see as many as three points and there were also one-half point increments.

S: So I am paying more for the mortgage?

P: Correct, and right at closing, which unfortunately is adding to your already significant closing costs.

S: So what was the decision to be made?

P: Well, using the hypothetical $200,000, let's say the lending institution offered a 30 year fixed rate mortgage for 4.3 percent or you could pay one point and get a 4 percent rate?

S: Let me handle the calculation here. If I pay the point and get a 4 percent rate, I am paying $2,000 up front. If I don't pay the point, I save the $2,000 up front, but my rate is 0.3 percent higher. What would that make my monthly mortgage payments?

P: They would now be approximately $990.

S: Okay, so that's $35 per month more. By paying the $2,000 up front, I am saving $35 per month so it would take me approximately 57 months (or four years and nine months) to recover the $2,000.

P: You are getting good at this.

S: So what's your advice?

P: It depends on a lot of factors, whether you can afford the extra dollars at closing, how long you think you will have the house or the loan, et cetera. All you can do is run the calculations and figure out what is best for you.

S: My parents and grandparents have told me they refinanced their homes a few times. Why would that occur?

P: People would refinance their homes when interest rates dropped. In the best of all worlds, in a refinancing, you could walk away with cash and a lower monthly payment even if you increased the amount you owed.

S: How could that happen?

P: You have seen the power, both positive and negative, of interest rates. I'll let you "run" the numbers on your own after we cover everything. The general rule of thumb is that if rates decreased by 2 percent or more, it was worth refinancing, but again everyone has to consider their individual facts and circumstances.

S: If I were to get a loan now, do you think I will be refinancing it some day?

P: Only if you need extra money. It won't be because of interest rates dropping around 2 percent. If they do, I'll give you another six strokes on the golf course...and you still won't beat me!

S: What was that last comment?

P: Nothing, you must be hearing things. You know how to run numbers. Later in your life, if you are into a mortgage at high rates and then rates decrease significantly, you know how to evaluate the possibility of refinancing.

S: I actually feel confident I could do that! I am afraid to ask this question, but tax aspects?

P: Take the class and you won't have to be afraid to ask questions about taxes. As of now, mortgage interest is deductible up to limits you don't need to worry about at this time. It is an itemized deductions on Schedule A. Property taxes are deductible, but must be combined with state and local income taxes and the total is subject to a $10,000 limit. Points are deductible for a purchased home. For a refinancing, the total must be amortized over the life of the loan.

S: I'll wait until tax class and then ask about the points.

P: Good move.

S: How about closing costs?

P: Give me a short break and then we will discuss those. In the meantime, I have attached some intervals within the first five years of an amortization schedule for a 30 year fixed rate mortgage at 4 percent (Table 4). Interest costs are far higher than the principal repaid each month in the first part of a mortgage, but the mix changes a little bit each month. Remember also what I told you about paying extra money if you have the means and don't see the need for the extra money paid in the foreseeable future. I have every confidence your yearly pay increases will outpace inflation.

TABLE 4

MORTGAGE BALANCE	$200,000
INTEREST RATE	4.000%
MONTHLY PAYMENT	$954.83 per month

MONTH	BALANCE	INTEREST	PAYMENT	END BALANCE	YEARLY INTEREST PAID	YEARLY PRINCIPAL PAID	TOTAL PAYMENTS
12	$196,776.84	$655.92	$954.83	$196,477.93	$7,935.89	$3,522.07	$11,457.96
24	$193,123.46	$643.74	$954.83	$192,812.37	$7,792.40	$3,665.56	$11,457.96
36	$189,321.23	$631.07	$954.83	$188,997.47	$7,643.06	$3,814.90	$11,457.96
48	$185,364.10	$617.88	$954.83	$185,027.15	$7,487.63	$3,970.33	$11,457.96
60	$181,245.74	$604.15	$954.83	$180,895.07	$7,325.88	$4,132.08	$11,457.96

MORTGAGE CLOSING

STUDENT: I have heard that closing costs can be significant. Can we run through what is involved in a mortgage closing?

PROFESSOR: Sure. A time and a place will be agreed for the closing. Your real estate agent should be accompanying you to the closing and you will need a certified check to cover the closing costs which will have been laid out in advance.

You'll sign a lot of papers which cover every aspect of the closing. I remember signing only a few when we closed on our house many years ago. Each refinancing brought more over the years and I think I counted 27 at the last refinancing.

S: Do I need to read them all in detail?

P: Many of them are short and self-explanatory, but make sure you ask questions if you don't understand any of them.

I have a copy of a mortgage closing here, which a financial institution was kind enough to share with me after redacting any identifiable information. The values are most likely larger than you will most likely have at your first closing, but the concepts remain the same.

Closing Disclosure

This form is a statement of final loan terms and closing costs. Compare this document with your Loan Estimate.

Closing Information		Transaction Information		Loan Information	
Date Issued	2/24/2017	**Borrower**		**Loan Term**	30 years
Closing Date	2/28/2017			**Purpose**	Purchase
Disbursement Date	2/28/2017			**Product**	10/1 Adjustable Rate
Settlement Agent		**Seller**		**Loan Type**	☒ Conventional ☐ FHA
File #					☐ VA ☐ _____
Property	See Addendum			**Loan ID #**	
		Lender		**MIC #**	
Sale Price	$832,500				

Loan Terms

		Can this amount increase after closing?
Loan Amount	$666,000	**NO**
Interest Rate	3.375%	**YES** · Adjusts **every year** starting in year 11. · Can go **as high as 9.375%** in year 13. · See **AIR Table on page 4** for details.
Monthly Principal & Interest *See Projected Payments below for your Estimated Total Monthly Payment*	$2,944.36	**YES** · Adjusts **every year** starting in year 11. · Can go **as high as $4,667** in year 13.
		Does the loan have these features?
Prepayment Penalty		**NO**
Balloon Payment		**NO**

Projected Payments

Payment Calculation	Years 1 - 10	Year 11	Year 12	Years 13 - 30
Principal & Interest	$2,944.36	$2,847 min $3,495 max	$2,847 min $4,072 max	$2,847 min $4,667 max
Mortgage Insurance	+ 0.00	+ 0.00	+ 0.00	+ 0.00
Estimated Escrow *Amount can increase over time*	+ 0.00	+ 0.00	+ 0.00	+ 0.00
Estimated Total Monthly Payment	$2,944.36	$2,847-$3,495	$2,847-$4,072	$2,847-$4,667

Estimated Taxes, Insurance & Assessments *Amount can increase over time* *See page 4 for details*	$824.27 a month	**This estimate includes** ☒ Property Taxes ☒ Homeowner's Insurance ☐ Other: *See Escrow Account on page 4 for details. You must pay for other property costs separately.*	**In escrow?** NO NO

Costs at Closing

Closing Costs	$11,857.64	Includes $3,231.20 in Loan Costs + $8,626.44 in Other Costs -$0 in Lender Credits. *See page 2 for details.*
Cash to Close	$167,706.33	Includes Closing Costs. *See Calculating Cash to Close on page 3 for details.*

Closing Cost Details

Loan Costs	Borrower-Paid		Seller-Paid		Paid by Others
	At Closing	Before Closing	At Closing	Before Closing	
A. Origination Charges	**$600.00**				
01 ___% of Loan Amount Points					
02 Application Fee to I'	$600.00				
03					
04					
05					
06					
07					
08					
B. Services Borrower Did Not Shop For	**$545.70**				
01 Appraisal Fee to '		$495.00			
02 Credit Report to	$36.70				
03 Flood Determination Fee to	$14.00				
04					
05					
06					
07					
08					
09					
C. Services Borrower Did Shop For	**$2,085.50**				
01 Title - Lender's Title Policy to "	$1,415.50				
02 Title - Settlement Fee to	$670.00				
03					
04					
05					
06					
07					
08					
D. TOTAL LOAN COSTS (Borrower-Paid)	**$3,231.20**				
Loan Costs Subtotals (A + B + C)	$2,736.20	$495.00			

Other Costs	Borrower-Paid		Seller-Paid		Paid by Others
E. Taxes and Other Government Fees	**$6,406.00**				
01 Recording Fees Deed: $41.00 Mortgage: $109.00	$162.00				
02 Transfer Taxes to Registry of Deeds	$6,244.00				
03 Transfer Taxes			$6,244.00		
F. Prepaids	**$1,582.44**				
01 Homeowner's Insurance Premium (12 mo.) to Hazard Company		$1,520.00			
02 Mortgage Insurance Premium (mo.)					
03 Prepaid Interest ($62.4375 per day from 2/28/17 to 3/1/17)	$62.44				
04 Property Taxes (mo.)					
05					
G. Initial Escrow Payment at Closing					
01 Homeowner's Insurance (per month for mo.)					
02 Mortgage Insurance (per month for mo.)					
03 Property Taxes (per month for mo.)					
04					
05					
06					
07					
08 Aggregate Adjustment					
H. Other	**$638.00**				
01 Document Preparation to			$175.00		
02 Final Water to I			$18.80		
03 Outgoing Wire Fee to			$25.00		
04 Overnight Discharge tracking fee to (			$99.00		
05 Real Estate Commission to			$18,731.25		
06 Real Estate Commission to			$18,731.25		
07 Title - Owner's Title Policy (optional) to '	$638.00				
08					
I. TOTAL OTHER COSTS (Borrower-Paid)	**$8,626.44**				
Other Costs Subtotals (E + F + G + H)	$7,106.44	$1,520.00			
J. TOTAL CLOSING COSTS (Borrower-Paid)	**$11,857.64**				
Closing Costs Subtotals (D + I)	$9,842.64	$2,015.00	$44,024.30		
Lender Credits					

Calculating Cash to Close

Use this table to see what has changed from your Loan Estimate.

	Loan Estimate	Final	Did this change?
Total Closing Costs (J)	$13,480.00	$11,857.64	**YES** • See **Total Loan Costs (D)** and **Total Other Costs (I)**
Closing Costs Paid Before Closing	$0.00	-$2,015.00	**YES** • You paid these Closing Costs **before closing.**
Closing Costs Financed (Paid from your Loan Amount)	$0.00	$0.00	**NO**
Down Payment/Funds from Borrower	$166,500.00	$166,500.00	**NO**
Deposit	-$10,000.00	-$10,000.00	**NO**
Funds for Borrower	$0.00	$0.00	**NO**
Seller Credits	$0.00	$0.00	**NO**
Adjustments and Other Credits	$0.00	$1,363.69	**YES** • See details in **Sections K and L.**
Cash to Close	$169,980.00	$167,706.33	

Summaries of Transactions

Use this table to see a summary of your transaction.

BORROWER'S TRANSACTION		SELLER'S TRANSACTION	
K. Due from Borrower at Closing	**$843,726.99**	**M. Due to Seller at Closing**	**$833,884.35**
01 Sale Price of Property	$832,500.00	01 Sale Price of Property	$832,500.00
02 Sale Price of Any Personal Property Included in Sale		02 Property Included in Sale	
03 Closing Costs Paid at Closing	$9,842.64	03	
04 Payoffs and Payments	$0.00	04	
Adjustments		05	
05		06	
06		07	
07		08	
Adjustments for Items Paid by Seller in Advance		**Adjustments for Items Paid by Seller in Advance**	
08 City/Town Taxes 2/28/17 to 3/31/17	$704.51	09 City/Town Taxes 2/28/17 to 3/31/17	$704.51
09 County Taxes to		10 County Taxes to	
10 Assessments to		11 Assessments to	
11 Oil Proration 247.5 gals. @2.39 to	$591.52	12 Oil Proration 247.5 gals. @2.39 to	$591.52
12 Propane proration 23 gals @ 3.84 to	$88.32	13 Propane proration 23 gals @ 3.84 to	$88.32
13		14	
14		15	
15		16	
L. Paid Already by or on Behalf of Borrower at Closing	**$676,020.66**	**N. Due from Seller at Closing**	**$44,086.96**
01 Deposit	$10,000.00	01 Excess Deposit	
02 Loan Amount	$666,000.00	02 Closing Costs Paid at Closing (J)	$44,024.30
03 Existing Loan(s) Assumed or Taken Subject to		03 Existing Loan(s) Assumed or Taken Subject to	
04 Subordinate Financing	$0.00	04 Payoff of First Mortgage Loan	
05 Seller Credit	$0.00	05 Payoff of Second Mortgage Loan	
Other Credits		06	
06		07	
07		08 Seller Credit	$0.00
Adjustments		09 Discharge Mortgage	$42.00
08		10	
09		11	
10		12	
11		13	
Adjustments for Items Unpaid by Seller		**Adjustments for Items Unpaid by Seller**	
12 City/Town Taxes to		14 City/Town Taxes to	
13 County Taxes to		15 County Taxes to	
14 Assessments to		16 Assessments to	
15 to	$20.66	17 to	$20.66
16		18	
17		19	
CALCULATION		**CALCULATION**	
Total Due from Borrower at Closing (K)	$843,726.99	Total Due to Seller at Closing (M)	$833,884.35
Total Paid Already by or on Behalf of Borrower at Closing (L)	-$676,020.66	Total Due from Seller at Closing (N)	-$44,086.96
Cash to Close ☒ From ☐ To Borrower	**$167,706.33**	**Cash** ☐ From ☒ To Seller	**$789,797.39**

Additional Information About This Loan

Loan Disclosures

Assumption
If you sell or transfer this property to another person, your lender
- ☐ will allow, under certain conditions, this person to assume this loan on the original terms.
- ☒ will not allow assumption of this loan on the original terms.

Demand Feature
Your loan
- ☐ has a demand feature, which permits your lender to require early repayment of the loan. You should review your note for details.
- ☒ does not have a demand feature.

Late Payment
If your payment is more than 15 days late, we will charge a late fee of 5% of the monthly principal and interest payment.

Negative Amortization (Increase in Loan Amount)
Under your loan terms, you
- ☐ are scheduled to make monthly payments that do not pay all of the interest due that month. As a result, your loan amount will increase (negatively amortize), and your loan amount will likely become larger than your original loan amount. Increases in your loan amount lower the equity you have in this property.
- ☐ may have monthly payments that do not pay all of the interest due that month. If you do, your loan amount will increase (negatively amortize), and, as a result, your loan amount may become larger than your original loan amount. Increases in your loan amount lower the equity you have in this property.
- ☒ do not have a negative amortization feature.

Partial Payments
Your lender
- ☒ may accept payments that are less than the full amount due (partial payments) and apply them to your loan.
- ☐ may hold them in a separate account until you pay the rest of the payment, and then apply the full payment to your loan.
- ☐ does not accept any partial payments.

If this loan is sold, your new lender may have a different policy.

Security Interest
You are granting a security interest in

You may lose this property if you do not make your payments or satisfy other obligations for this loan.

Escrow Account
For now, your loan
- ☐ will have an escrow account (also called an "impound" or "trust" account) to pay the property costs listed below. Without an escrow account, you would pay them directly, possibly in one or two large payments a year. Your lender may be liable for penalties and interest for failing to make a payment.

Escrow		
Escrowed Property Costs over Year 1		Estimated total amount over year 1 for your escrowed property costs:
Non-Escrowed Property Costs over Year 1		Estimated total amount over year 1 for your non-escrowed property costs:
		You may have other property costs.
Initial Escrow Payment		A cushion for the escrow account you pay at closing. See Section G on page 2.
Monthly Escrow Payment		The amount included in your total monthly payment.

- ☒ will not have an escrow account because ☒ you declined it ☐ your lender does not offer one. You must directly pay your property costs, such as taxes and homeowner's insurance. Contact your lender to ask if your loan can have an escrow account.

No Escrow		
Estimated Property Costs over Year 1	$9,066.97	Estimated total amount over year 1. You must pay these costs directly, possibly in one or two large payments a year.
Escrow Waiver Fee		

In the future,
Your property costs may change and, as a result, your escrow payment may change. You may be able to cancel your escrow account, but if you do, you must pay your property costs directly. If you fail to pay your property taxes, your state or local government may (1) impose fines and penalties or (2) place a tax lien on this property. If you fail to pay any of your property costs, your lender may (1) add the amounts to your loan balance, (2) add an escrow account to your loan, or (3) require you to pay for property insurance that the lender buys on your behalf, which likely would cost more and provide fewer benefits than what you could buy on your own.

Adjustable Interest Rate (AIR) Table

Index + Margin	Treasury Bill + 3%
Initial Interest Rate	3.375%
Minimum/Maximum Interest Rate	3%/9.375%
Change Frequency	
First Change	Beginning of 121st month
Subsequent Changes	Every 12th month after first change
Limits on Interest Rate Changes	
First Change	2%
Subsequent Changes	2%

Loan Calculations

Total of Payments. Total you will have paid after you make all payments of principal, interest, mortgage insurance, and loan costs, as scheduled.	$1,095,120.03
Finance Charge. The dollar amount the loan will cost you.	$426,502.83
Amount Financed. The loan amount available after paying your upfront finance charge.	$665,323.56
Annual Percentage Rate (APR). Your costs over the loan term expressed as a rate. This is not your interest rate.	3.577%
Total Interest Percentage (TIP). The total amount of interest that you will pay over the loan term as a percentage of your loan amount.	63.947%

Questions? If you have questions about the loan terms or costs on this form, use the contact information below. To get more information or make a complaint, contact the Consumer Financial Protection Bureau at **www.consumerfinance.gov/mortgage-closing**

Other Disclosures

Appraisal
If the property was appraised for your loan, your lender is required to give you a copy at no additional cost at least 3 days before closing. If you have not yet received it, please contact your lender at the information listed below.

Contract Details
See your note and security instrument for information about
- what happens if you fail to make your payments,
- what is a default on the loan,
- situations in which your lender can require early repayment of the loan, and
- the rules for making payments before they are due.

Liability after Foreclosure
If your lender forecloses on this property and the foreclosure does not cover the amount of unpaid balance on this loan,
- ☐ state law may protect you from liability for the unpaid balance. If you refinance or take on any additional debt on this property, you may lose this protection and have to pay any debt remaining even after foreclosure. You may want to consult a lawyer for more information.
- ☒ state law does not protect you from liability for the unpaid balance.

Refinance
Refinancing this loan will depend on your future financial situation, the property value, and market conditions. You may not be able to refinance this loan.

Tax Deductions
If you borrow more than this property is worth, the interest on the loan amount above this property's fair market value is not deductible from your federal income taxes. You should consult a tax advisor for more information.

Contact Information

	Lender	Real Estate Broker (B)	Real Estate Broker (S)	Settlement Agent
Name				
Address				
NMLS ID				
License ID				
Contact				
Contact NMLS ID				
Contact License ID				
Email				
Phone				

Confirm Receipt

By signing, you are only confirming that you have received this form. You do not have to accept this loan because you have signed or received this form.

_____ Date   _____ Date

S: Well it doesn't look as bad as I thought it would be, though there are a heck of a lot of numbers there.

P: There certainly are but, based on our previous discussions, I think you are going to understand much of it. I'll tell you what, you start reviewing the document and explain as much as you can to me starting with the first page.

S: Let's see, the borrower, the seller, and the property are identified. The sales price is $832,500…yeah, you said that is probably a little bit more than my first house will be. It is a 30 year loan under a 10/1 conventional ARM.

The buyer is borrowing $666,000 and the interest rate is 3.375 percent. Wow, based on the rates we looked at, rates have already gone up.

P: Good catch and, as discussed, I think they will continue to go up. You're doing a nice job, but explain the 10/1 to me.

S: The rate of 3.375 percent is fixed for 10 years; after that it will adjust each year. It can go as high as 9.375 percent which means the overall cap is 6 percent. I can't identify any annual cap yet but I'll guess it is 2 percent.

P: I don't see it yet either but keep going, I like that our prior discussions are paying dividends.

S: Well, the monthly P&I is $2,944; wow it can go as high as $4,667 in year 13…and that is after they have already made principal payments for 12 years. That's frightening. Oh, now I see where they factor in increases under the ARM. The payments can rise to $3,495 in year 11, $4,072 in year 12, and then $4,667 in year 13 and beyond if rates rise enough. Just looking at the increase from year 10 to year 11, that is unbelievable that all of a sudden you are paying $551 ($3,495 - $2,944) more just because of interest rate changes.

P: Yes it is. Remember I told you that, at this time, I'd only take an ARM under certain circumstances. I have to believe the borrowers here are planning on selling in less than 10 years.

S: Okay, then I see that the estimated monthly property taxes and homeowners insurance are $824 per month. Wow, that is another $9,888 per year.

P: Based on the home value, I actually thought it would be more.

S: What does the "in escrow" mean?

P: Great question. When you purchase your first home, you will most likely have to pay for a year of homeowners insurance in advance and you'll have to pay for property taxes up to the date of purchase. You'll find these shortly. To ensure that you will pay the property taxes to the city or town when they are next due, and that you continue to have money available for the second year of homeowners insurance, your monthly payment will be increased to cover those two costs. The money will be placed in an escrow account. This is an account maintained by your lender and they will make those payments when they become due.

S: How do they figure out how much extra to charge me?

P: They know the current property taxes and homeowners insurance so they adjust those for projected increases.

S: What if they are wrong? And do they pay me interest when they are holding my money to make payments on my behalf?

P: They will be wrong; it is just a forecast. As I like to say in class, in any situation a forecast of sales, expenses, et cetera will be wrong; it is just trying to minimize how wrong it is. The number will be readjusted each year at a minimum.

As for interest, they will certainly pay interest, but do you think you'll be getting a lot?

S: Based on the savings interest rates that we saw, it will be "chump change."

P: You are correct and glad to see you are picking up some of the lingo. What else can you tell me?

S: Well the closing costs will be $11,857.64 and it says to turn to page two. You told me there are closing costs for the buyer and seller. Are these the total for both of them?

P: No, based on what you've looked at so far, whose do you think they are?

S: Well everything has pertained to the buyer so far so I will say the buyer.

P: Your logic is great, let's turn the page and see what makes up the $11k+.

S: Let's see…We have the origination fee of $600…what is that?

P: It is a fee paid either to the lending institution—which would have been discussed well in advance—or if the buyer used a mortgage broker, it may be the fee paid to the mortgage broker.

S: There is an appraisal fee of $495 which was paid before the closing. Why do I need an appraisal, and if it is paid before the closing, am I paying it again at the closing?

P: Think like a lender now. Using illustrative numbers, when you have money in the future, your friend asks if he can borrow $40,000 for a Ford Escort. Would you lend it to him or her?

S: That would be foolish, the Escort only goes for $16,000 and if I need to repossess it, I will be out quite a bit of money. Now thinking logically, if a house is appraised for $250,000, why would the bank ever loan $300,000? Okay, I got this concept.

Let's see if I can figure out my second question...I got it. If I look at the bottom of page two, I see the $11,857.64 is broken down into $9,842.64 paid at the closing and $2,015 paid before the closing. Okay, I see because $2,015 has been paid before the closing, "only" $9,842.64 is due at the closing.

P: Nice work. What else do you see?

S: Well looks like a credit report on the borrower costs $36.70 and there is a flood determination fee of $14. What is this?

P: The $14 is to determine if the property is in a flood zone which would require additional homeowners insurance coverage. We'll go through homeowners insurance next.

S: What are these title costs?

P: You'll be required to buy title insurance which covers the mortgage amount if the title to the property happens to be defective. If it is defective, you are not the legal owner. The $1,415.50 covers the lender for the amount of the mortgage due if the title is defective. The $670 covers the research work done by the title company

S: What could cause it to be defective, and how often does this happen?

P: It could be due to a filing error in the records department at City Hall, an unpaid lien (money due secured by the property that was not discovered), an unexpected heir, or a variety of other reasons. It does not happen a lot, but it would be devastating if it did as you have borrowed money against something you do not legally own.

S: Even I can understand that would be ugly. Okay, recording fees to note my ownership and the mortgage against the property are $162. What about the transfer taxes of $6,244?

P: That is a tax the state of New Hampshire charges on transfers of property. The $6,244 is 0.75 percent of the sales price of $832,500. It is paid by both the buyer and the seller.

S: Prepaid interest of $62.44?

P: Mortgages are set up so the payment is due on the first of the month and you normally have until the fifteenth before you are late with the payment. Interest thus has to be paid from the date of the closing until the first of the month.

S: I can see the dating on the closing document. Does that mean if they closed on the first of February, then $1,748 would be due as prepaid interest? ($62.4375 * 28)

P: You are getting really good at understanding how things fit together.

S: Then you have another title insurance fee of $638. What is this?

P: This is the option of the buyer to purchase owner's title insurance to cover their interest in the property as long as they own the property, even if the mortgage is paid off.

S: Between the three title insurances, that is a lot of money. Are you sure a title is not defective often?

P: Not often. I read an article years ago that said title insurance companies keep 93% of the premiums paid. (Woolley, 2006). You can search for lower cost title insurance but make sure you do your due diligence in this area.

Moving to the top of page three now, this is a document that provides a detailed analysis of the changes between the estimated closing costs and the actual closing costs. It is a good summary so the borrower can see the changes in the costs.

S: Okay, I am following fairly well, but I have no idea where the $843,726.99 "due from borrower" in the Summaries of Transactions comes from. Can you help me here?

P: Sure, not the easiest to follow, but the price of the house is $832,500, the closing costs due now—that you already figured out for me—are $9,842.64. Add to these two, one month's worth of property taxes for $704.51. Looks like the seller has paid property taxes through March 31; as the buyer is buying on February 28, the buyer needs to reimburse the seller for the last day of February and all of March.

It looks like there are 247.5 gallons left in the oil tank at $2.39 per gallon and 23 gallons of propane left at $3.84 per gallon for another $679.84 to be added.

S: Wait a minute!! How do I check I am not getting ripped off here?

P: You can bang the oil tank if you wish or pay someone to get you an exact measurement and request receipts for the last purchase; however I would recommend you accept these numbers in good faith. If you are paying $832,500 for a house, you want the house, and why potentially derail it over relatively minor amounts? Hopefully you have met the seller and have developed a good rapport with him or her. You'll be selling some day and requesting some amounts for these, and I know you will act in good faith.

S: Okay, I am following it. So the buyer "owes" $843,726.99 for all costs we have discussed. The buyer put down a $10,000 deposit and is getting a loan for $666,000 which we already saw on page one. The seller has left some item unpaid for $20.66 so the buyer is getting credited for that thus the buyer "owes" $843,726.99 minus the deposit minus the loan amount minus the $20.66, so the buyer has to have cash of $167,706.33.

P: I wouldn't recommend bringing cash to the transaction. Nothing good can come from having that much cash in your possession. The buyer would have a certified check payable to the lender or some other agreed way to have the money in the lender's hands at the closing.

S: Wow, you weren't kidding when you said there were a lot of costs involved in a closing.

P: This doesn't pick up all that you will face. The buyer must have a good credit history and good track record with the bank. Do you remember one thing I told you that you would have to pay a year in advance?

S: Yes, the homeowner's insurance and I don't see that here.

P: Excellent, and remember that points may arise again in the future.

S: Refresh my mind as to what points are?

P: One percent of the loan amount.

S: So if the borrower took a loan and paid two points, the borrower would have had to pay another $13,320 ($666,000 * 2%). *Wow!!* I will keep my fingers crossed that points don't come into play again for quite some time.

I understand the buyer's side now. I will most likely also be a seller one day. Can you help me with the seller's side?

P: Once again, you are capable of doing this.

S: Well, let's see...the sales price is $832,500, we have already discussed the seller being reimbursed for the property taxes through the end of March and the remaining oil and propane. These total $1,384.35, so adding that to the $832,500 brings the amount due to seller to a total of $833,884.35.

Now the seller has closing costs of $44,024.30. Let me think...I saw this on page two. Wait a minute, they have doubled up the transfer taxes of $6,244.

P: The seller wishes they had made a mistake here but the transfer tax of 0.75 percent is payable by both the buyer and seller.

S: Wow, the state must like a lot of real estate activity!

P: Never a bad thing for the state for sure but…also good for you and me as we pay neither income taxes nor sales taxes in New Hampshire.

S: Let me see what else is there on page two. There is a document preparation fee of $175, the final water bill, or at least it looks like that for $18.80, a wire transfer fee for $25 and an overnight discharge fee for $99.

P: Yes, that is not the final water bill as the monthly bill will be far higher than $18.80, but maybe it is some portion of the final bill. There will be all sorts of relatively small costs that will be advised to the seller well before the closing.

S: Wow, did they duplicate the real estate commission? I see $18,731.25 twice.

P: No, in real estate, the buyer's brokerage firm gets one-half and the seller's agency gets one-half. Let's see you figure out what the commission percentage paid on the sale is.

S: Well $18,731.25 times two gives me $37,462.50. If I divide the $37,462.50 by the selling price of $832,500, that is 4.5 percent. Wow!! They got a great deal with a real estate commission of 4.5 percent.

P: I'm not sure of that. This is one of those areas where you are never quite sure.

S: Are you kidding? You told me the normal commission is around 6 percent.

P: Yes, I did but a house selling for this much has significant built-in value. Let's say they could have sold it without an agent for $750,000.

S: Well they are still receiving more using the agent.

P: What if they could have sold it without the agent for $825,000?

S: Okay, in that case, they are better off without the agent.

P: From a purely financial standpoint for sure, but the unanswered question is how much time and effort would it take on the part of the owners and what other incremental costs would they have by doing it themselves?

S: So you are telling me there is no correct answer.

P: Voila! Most people are better off using an agent who has the skills, advertising, et cetera to more easily market and show the house, but it is a decision that is best made by the individual as to the best approach.

S: Okay, so going back to page three of the closing statement, the seller has the closing costs of $44,024.30, there is a $42 fee to discharge the mortgage, and the seller has to reimburse the buyer for the $20.66 that we stated before. The seller thus has total closing costs of $44,086.96. If we subtract that from the amount due to the seller we previously calculated of $833,844.35, the seller is due a balance of $789,797.39. *Wow!*

P: Hopefully if they are getting a check, they are headed to the bank after the closing, or they are having the money wired there from the bank.

S: Selling for $789k, there has to be tax implications for sure.

P: Maybe, maybe not, but you know what the answer here is.

S: Take the tax course.

P: You got it. There are all sorts of possibilities with respect to the sale of a home. I will say that for most people, the sale of a home is tax free, but you need to know the specific rules for sure.

S: What's next? Let me guess, we have bought the home and after covering buying a car, we talked about car insurance so we must now need to talk about homeowners insurance.

P: You'll be ready to explain all this to someone else down the line without a doubt.

HOMEOWNERS INSURANCE

STUDENT: I am ready to go through homeowners insurance. You have given me the first page of a policy here which looks pretty basic. I see there is a deductible of $500 which, if the same as auto insurance, means that I have to pay the first $500 of any covered loss.

PROFESSOR: Excellent.

S: And I see they give the policy holder three alternatives, so risk versus reward is once again coming into play. If this policy holder wants to increase their deductible to $1,000, they will save $98, with a $2,500 deductible they will save $257, and with a $5,000 deductible they will save $386. What is the best alternative?

P: You can surely answer this one.

S: Well based on everything we have spoken about to date, it is whatever the individual feels is best for himself or herself. There are many different views towards risk and reward and it is whatever each individual is most comfortable with.

Amica

MICHAEL J. MC GUINNESS AND
MARY A. MC GUINNESS

IMPORTANT CHANGES TO YOUR HOMEOWNERS RENEWAL POLICY

Our records indicate the coverage limit of your home needs to be adjusted. We are increasing your dwelling coverage to   in line with our estimate.

Many factors went into estimating your dwelling limit. One of these factors is reconstruction costs. Reconstruction costs have risen steadily since our last survey of your home. We consider various other factors during our valuation process that impact the dwelling amount. If you have questions or comments, we welcome your input. You may contact your local Amica office to discuss this further or to request changes to the dwelling coverage limit at any time during the policy period.

You likely have the desire to insure your home at a limit reflecting its actual reconstruction cost at today's prices while minimizing your premium payments. Many of our insureds elect a higher deductible to accomplish both goals. Please consider the following options:

Current Deductible: $500

Option 1 Revised Deductible: $1,000   Estimated Savings: $98
Option 2 Revised Deductible: $2,500   Estimated Savings: $257
Option 3 Revised Deductible: $5,000   Estimated Savings: $386

If you would like to take advantage of the savings illustrated or discuss other coverage options, please contact your local branch office. It is important to remember that ultimately you are responsible for determining the proper value of your dwelling. In the event you fail to maintain sufficient coverage, your insurance policy may not provide adequate limits to replace your home in the event of a total loss. Dwelling coverage is limited to 130% of the Coverage A limit. Your local branch office would welcome discussing your dwelling's value and can employ estimating tools to help with your decision.

Also, please remember to inform us within 30 days of any dwelling alterations which increase the replacement cost of your dwelling by 5% or more.

AMICA MUTUAL INSURANCE COMPANY
LINCOLN, RHODE ISLAND

DECLARATIONS

HOMEOWNERS POLICY NO.

NAMED INSURED AND MAILING ADDRESS
MICHAEL J. MC GUINNESS AND
MARY A. MC GUINNESS

POLICY PERIOD: 12:01 A.M., Standard Time at the residence premises

From: AUGUST 5, 2017
To: AUGUST 5, 2018

ROCKINGHAM
County in which premises is located

The residence premises covered by this policy is located at the above address unless otherwise stated:

COVERAGE IS PROVIDED WHERE A PREMIUM OR LIMIT OF LIABILITY IS SHOWN FOR THE COVERAGE			
Section I Coverages	**Limit of Liability**		**Premium**
A. Dwelling	$	Basic Policy	$
B. Other Structures	$		$
C. Personal Property	$	WORKERS' COMP.	$
D. Loss of Use	$	SELECTED COVERAGES	$
Section II Coverages			$
E. Personal Liability	$ Each Occurrence	TOTAL PREMIUM	$
F. Medical Payments to Others	$ Each Person		

DEDUCTIBLE-SECTION I : $500

SPECIAL DISCOUNT:
MULTI-LINE CREDIT
AGE OF HOME/REMODELED HOME CR

Special State Provisions:

Section II - Other insured locations:

Mortgagee

This policy shall not be valid unless countersigned by our authorized agent or representative.

Authorized Representative

Policy Number:
Effective Date: AUGUST 5, 2017

Dear Policyholder:

Please accept our sincere appreciation for insuring with Amica. Maintaining your trust and confidence continues to be our highest priority.

Your renewal policy as well as related materials and necessary information are enclosed. Please review the Information Digest for important coverage descriptions and options.

The following is either required by law or included in further explanation of your renewal policy.

Our records indicate that you are currently receiving the following protective device credits on your policy:

FIRE ALARM: SMOKE DETECTOR(S)
BURGLAR ALARM: NONE
INTERIOR SPRINKLERS: NO

If your protective device credits need to be updated, please notify us as soon as possible.

Please note that a bill is not included with your policy package. The bill will be delivered to you closer to your policy effective date and approximately 20 days before your payment due date. If you are currently receiving paper bills, you have the option of signing up for electronic billing through our website at Amica.com.

Millions of people are victims of identity theft every year. Amica's Identity Fraud expense coverage provides up to $15,000 for repairing identity theft problems, subject to a $500 deductible. We've partnered with Identity Theft 911, a recognized leader in resolution and education. Their experts will guide you through the process of repairing your personal identity. Please contact us for more information.

Your policy doesn't provide coverage for damage caused by water that backs up through sewers or drains or overflows from a sump. You can add this coverage at a limit of $5,000 with a $500 deductible for an estimated additional cost of $ 45.00.

Additional limits and deductible options are available. Please see the enclosed Information Digest or contact us to learn more.

AUTO   HOME   LIFE

P: You are ready to teach this course.

S: Not quite yet, but let's go through the policy page.

Section 1A covers the dwelling. Can I use hypothetical numbers here to discuss insurance?

P: Absolutely, this is the best way to discuss this. Your dwelling limit should be based on the replacement value of your home so give me a number as to what your home would cost to rebuild.

S: I will say $300,000 which, if I am following things correctly, means I have $300,000 of coverage on my house.

P: That is correct and if there are any attachments to your house such as a garage, the attachments are covered also.

S: Got it. What about the "other structures" section in this document?

P: This section covers unattached structures on your property such as an unattached garage, a storage shed, et cetera.

S: The insurance company can't possibly provide $300,000 of coverage on a garage, storage shed, or other structure.

P: You are absolutely correct again. This will be limited to a percentage of the coverage on the dwelling. Normally it is 10 percent, meaning that any other structures not attached to your home have $30,000 ($300,000 * 10%) of coverage.

S: So personal property is probably some percentage of the Section A coverage also then? What percentage might that be?

P: Well. We'll look at this two ways. The Insurance Services Organization ("ISO") writes standardized policy and endorsement language that are followed by a large number of insurance companies. We'll look at their standards as well as the provisions of this specific policy. The ISO language is for 50 percent of the dwelling coverage for personal property, while this policy covers 75 percent.

S: So at 50 percent I would have $150,000 of personal property coverage, and at 75 percent I would have $225,000 of personal property coverage?

P: Yes you would, however there are going to be limits on different categories of personal property.

S: Such as?

P: Well, I'll give you a few examples. Again, each policy may be a bit different so I'll use numbers associated with this policy. Cash is limited to $200…

S: *What!!* Are you kidding me? If I have a good day at Mohegan Sun and have $1,500 in cash and my house gets broken into that night, I only get reimbursed for $200?

P: That is correct. Going back to risk/reward, I hope you appreciate the odds are not in your favor on each individual casino trip. Those luxury towers have not been built because people are winning a lot of money. Any time you go to a casino, consider any money that you return with as winnings. That said, if you are going to go, play blackjack. That game has the smallest percent in the casino's favor.

Seriously though, think about it, if there was no limit on cash claims, anything greater leads to the risk of insurance fraud, which leads to higher premiums for everyone.

There is a $1,500 limit on watercraft of all types including all associated equipment (i.e. motors, trailers, et cetera).

Two other examples are a $1,500 limit on losses of jewelry, watches, furs, precious and semiprecious stones, and $2,500 for loss of silverware, gold-ware, platinum-ware, and other related valuables.

S: What if there is a $10,000 fur coat for which the value can be proven?

P: You will get $1,500 for it. For any very valuable items (other than cash), you can buy what is called a floater or rider. It comes with an additional premium but will then cover the loss up to the item's cost. Once you have a policy, see what your policy limitations are and then determine what property you might want to purchase a floater and request a premium quote. You know the trade-off!

S: Risk versus reward.

P: Certainly. I hate to have it being viewed as a reward, but the concept remains.

S: What about my personal property while I am traveling?

P: You have coverage for that at all times. However, coverage is limited to 10 percent of the coverage for personal property or $1,000, whichever is greater. This covers property stored at a residence other than the insured home, such as a vacation home. It also covers property stolen from a hotel not covered by any hotel insurance.

S: So we are talking about $1,000.

P: I'd be shocked if it was anything else and this also includes property located at storage facilities so, if you are using a storage facility, check to see what their insurance covers. The ISO is currently changing this. Older editions of insurance coverage had storage covered in full. The newest editions of insurance coverage may not. You need to check the policy or ask your agent.

S: Always questions, questions, questions!

P: Correct again but you know that is your best way of learning and…besides the questions, read the documentation. Remember, going back to purchasing a car or any item of significant value, whatever the salesperson is telling you they will cover is great, but if that is not consistent with the contract, unless you are ready for an expensive legal battle which you may not win, the contract prevails.

S: Got it. What is loss of use?

P: Before we cover it, give me a guess based on the term and what the coverage might be.

S: It has to cover expenses you incur if you can't live in the house due to a covered loss and it must be based on some percentage of the dwelling coverage.

P: Excellent! If you are unable to live in your house, it will cover any necessary increase in living expenses incurred by you so that your household can maintain its normal standard of living. Standard ISO is 20 percent, this policy provides coverage for up to 30 percent of the dwelling coverage.

S: Great! I always wanted to stay in a Four Seasons. If anything ever happens to my house, you'll find me there and having gourmet meals.

P: You deserve that, but just be ready to pay some of that bill yourself. I am guessing that is not your normal standard of living. You'll get reimbursed for some of it but you'll be battling the insurance company for sure. Remember I and other policyholders don't want you driving up our rates.

S: How long do I get to stay somewhere?

P: For the shortest time required to repair or replace the damage. The insurance company is reasonable here. They have adjusters who will work with the contractor who is repairing the damage and will work out a reasonable time frame. You won't have any issues with this coverage as long as you don't try to abuse it.

S: Anything else covered in Section I besides what we have already discussed?

P: A whole host of things are covered, subject to limitations, for damage caused by perils that are insured against.

S: Huh?

P: Your policy will discuss the perils or factors that can cause a loss to your property. There are named-peril policies that cover only those perils named in the policy, and then there are open-peril policies which cover all perils except those specifically excluded. Most policies are open-peril policies for dwelling, other structures, and loss of use; named-perils are personal property. You'll want to make sure you know your specific policy.

S: Wow is my head spinning again. What is the largest excluded area?

P: I'll come back to that in a minute. First, I'll give you a few examples of other types of items covered if the damage is caused by a covered peril. Again, there is a whole host of them but these serve as good illustrations.

Your insurance will generally cover debris removal, reasonable repairs to protect against further damage before the primary work can begin, trees, shrubs, and other plants. Also up to $500 if fire department charges are incurred or $500 for unauthorized use of your credit cards. I will reiterate again though, these have to be caused by a covered peril. Theft is always a covered peril unless it is a very unique policy.

The largest excluded area is flood insurance. Damage by flood is not covered unless it is specifically insured against. I would recommend getting flood insurance.

S: I live in an area that never floods so I am not going to worry about that.

P: Well, two things here. Never say never with respect to insurance; those All State commercials are pretty good and I've been told that over 50 percent of all flood claims happen in non-flood areas. What generally accompanies a hurricane?

S: High winds and significant rain.

P: And what can significant rain cause?

S: I got it.

P: One of the biggest dispute areas in insurance relates to hurricanes. What caused the damage, the wind or the water? From your standpoint, it was clearly the wind, a covered peril. From the standpoint of the insurance company, it may be the water which is flooding, a non-covered peril. Research some business articles after a major hurricane and I'll be surprised if you don't find the wind versus water conflict being discussed.

S: So what is your recommendation?

P: Know your options and I am confident you will make the best decision.

S: What about earthquakes? I have heard those are not covered.

P: Your information is correct. Earthquakes protection would be an addition to the policy. I heard a story recently from a woman in California who suffered $105,000 in damage after an earthquake in the area. She was shocked and quite disappointed to realize, after the fact, that she had a $100,000 deductible on earthquake coverage.

S: So she was reimbursed $5,000 for $105,000 of damage. What a rip-off!

P: Know your policy provisions. I can't blame her for that. I probably would not have not known that either which would be an error on my part.

S: Let's continue on, what does the personal liability cover?

P: If someone is injured on your property, or if you are responsible for injuries or property damage anywhere in the world, which is not excluded, you will be covered. For instance, you are traveling across the country and your little dachshund decides to take a nip out of a boy in Nebraska, you should be covered.

The insurance company will decide whether to settle (i.e. pay the requesting party) or defend against the claim. This is the insurance company's call. You want to have high coverage here; I would recommend $300,000 at a minimum here and, as you accumulate more assets, I strongly recommend an umbrella policy.

S: Well, I know that is a policy not designed to buy you an umbrella in the case of rain.

P: Not bad, but I won't use it in class. An umbrella policy covers amounts in excess of the coverage on your other policies. It is dirt cheap. You can most likely get $1,000,000 of coverage for $200–$250.

S: Why such a high amount on an umbrella policy?

P: We have a very litigious society and you never know what might be paid out. I also want to make you aware of what is referred to as an "attractive nuisance."

S: What, pray tell, is an attractive nuisance?

P: It is something such as a trampoline, ice skating rink, swimming pool, to which a younger person would be naturally attracted. Let's say you have a trampoline on your property for your kids and no one is home. Your 12-year-old neighbor comes on your property, bounces up and down, and severely injures him/herself in the process. There is a good chance your policy may be paying and your coverage may not be high enough.

S: But he was trespassing! I or my kids never invited him or her on the property.

P: I am not saying it is right or wrong, but a minor was severely injured on your property for which you can potentially be liable.

S: I don't think I will get any play equipment for my kids.

P: No need to do that, but just be aware of issues. I am not telling you not to get a trampoline or other items for your kids; just be aware of the risks.

S: What about medical payments to others?

P: Normally this is a very small amount to cover nuisance injuries to other people on your property. It is generally limited to $1,000. The thought is that most guests on your property don't want to sue you and if your policy covers their ambulance ride and tests, they won't. Unlike personal liability which we just discussed, you do not have to be negligent for medical payments to apply. Let's say your buddy has 23 beers and trips on your steps; this coverage would be available. It is generally limited to $1,000 but, like everything else, higher levels are available. Remember, you have the overall liability coverage.

S: I understand, but why did you say 23 beers?

P: Well, if your buddy is arrested, there is not enough to make a case.

S: That was pretty bad. Now on the right side, I see the premium and there are two other amounts for worker's compensation and selected coverages.

P: When you have outside contractors work on your house, you want to ask them if they are insured in the event that they cause injuries or cause damage to your property. I would not recommend dealing with a contractor that is not insured.

The workers comp covers people working on your property who may not be insured or are doing minor work on your property.

S: Do I ask to see their insurance coverage?

P: Your call. The contractors I have used for major projects have voluntarily shown their insurance coverage. You can request a Certificate of Insurance listing you as the certificate holder so you know the coverage is in force. I would not recommend a generic or photo copy. If the job is significant enough, you can request to be added as an "additional insured" to further protect you. It is not a bad idea as there is too much at stake if they are not insured.

S: Selected coverages?

P: Remember those floaters or riders I discussed?

S: Yes, they provide additional coverage where the policy limit is not high enough.

P: Very good. I had to buy this many, many years ago so my wife would not think she received a cubic zirconium ring and I have never remembered to cancel it. Glad I reviewed this with you, I can save myself a few dollars per year.

S: Glad I could help. Anything else?

P: Well, just look at the bottom of the page we just reviewed. You'll see the $500 deductible and the multi-line credit (Flo's Progressive bundling) because I have auto and life policies with them. We did do some remodeling quite a few years ago which saves me a little money also.

S: Can we go back to the page where the deductibles are? I see they increased your dwelling coverage in line with their estimates. Why do you let them increase your cost for that?

P: You want to make sure you have that in your policy. Construction costs generally rise with at least the rate of inflation each year—and sometimes much higher—so you want your insurance increasing so you have sufficient coverage. Note also, the last sentence on that page. If you are doing renovations, let your insurance company know contemporaneously so you have sufficient coverage. You do have a 30-day grace period, but I would be letting them know as the work starts at the latest.

I have also given you one additional page that provides for some additional coverages, the primary one being for helping you with identity theft.

S: What about this sewer back-up?

P: One of a homeowner's worst nightmares. You can see the coverage offered would not even begin to cover the damage here.

S: Can I sue the city or town?

P: Good luck with that. I don't like your chances there. Earlier you mentioned that you wanted to discuss the exciting stuff like stocks, bonds, and mutual funds. We'll get away from insurances for a bit to give you a break, before coming back to life and disability insurance.

INVESTING BASICS – STOCKS

STUDENT: We already talked about savings accounts and know that I understand interest rates, the value of compounding, et cetera, but I am very disappointed in the interest that I can earn at a bank or credit union.

PROFESSOR: I can't say that I blame you as rates are much lower than they historically have been. That said, you can borrow at rates which are historically low, so like many areas in business and finance, it depends on what side of the equation you are on.

S: Well my friends have taken this investment course and tell me you can make a fortune in the stock market.

P: You can do well for sure if you pick the right stocks. What is the one axiom with respect to investing I have tried to get you to fully understand?

S: The more the potential reward, the more the risk, and vice versa.

P: Excellent, I will cover three basic investments with you: stocks, bonds, and mutual funds. I will also cover them in that order although most young people early in their investing career should be in mutual funds, which is often the first topic covered. Since stocks and bonds make up a significant percentage of the assets of many mutual funds, a basic understanding of those will give you a better appreciation for mutual funds.

I am covering just the bare basics with you and would recommend you take the investments course which will go into far more detail than we can cover in our limited time.

S: Sounds good, I will look into that course. So, what stocks should I buy?

P: I have no recommendations, I am only explaining the basics to you so I'll start with the basic categories of stocks. You'll see different categories in different readings, but these are generally included

A *blue chip stock* is the first kind I'll cover.

These are strong companies with a long history and generally pay stable dividends. They are considered to be the best of the best.

S: What is a dividend?

P: There are various types of dividends but, by far, the most common is a regular return of profit to the shareholders. Companies that pay dividends generally pay them on a quarterly basis (every three months) although some pay them semi-annually (twice per year) or annually.

There are also *growth* stocks. It is believed that the earnings of these companies will outperform the average of the market.

Please note that companies move between categories. For example, Microsoft for years would have been considered a growth company but would now be considered a blue chip. General Electric would have been a blue chip for years whereas now it would probably be a special situation stock. Remember we talked about dividends. General Electric reduced its dividend from 31 cents per share in the second quarter of 2009, to 10 cents per share. (Glader and Laise, 2009). Over the last eight years, it gradually rose to 24 cents per share, but for its upcoming January 2018 payment has been cut again to 12 cents per share. (Gryta, 2017 November)

S: So if I owned 100 shares back in the first quarter of 2009, I would have received $31, then in the second quarter, I would have got $10. Wow, that is lousy.

P: No guarantee with respect to dividends, but I'll discuss them more a bit later.

There are *emerging growth companies* which are young companies in new industries that are good growth prospects. Facebook would have been an emerging growth company when going public but would now, most likely, be a growth company.

S: What do you mean by going public?

P: When a company goes public, it means that anybody can buy its stock. It has an initial public offering (IPO) on its first day. You can buy it at any time after it starts trading, although I would warn you about buying it on the first day. We'll discuss that later if you have time.

S: How do I buy the stock?

P: You would set up an account with an investment company like Fidelity, Putnam, Vanguard, et cetera. You deposit the money and then you can buy any company you want as long as you have sufficient funds in the account. You should be able to do this with the click of a keypad if you have set up your account correctly.

S: Sounds too easy.

P: It is easy as long as you have the money in the account. I won't get into buying on margin with you as you will learn that and much more in the investments course.

S: My friends in investments told me about market orders, but I didn't really understand them.

P: A market order means the investment company will buy it for you at the available market price.

S: Are there other types of orders?

P: Yes but I'll just cover two basic ones with you, limit orders and stop-loss orders. A limit order is used in combination with other trading strategies well beyond the scope of what you would be doing. Individuals sometimes use it when they think the stock is going up, but they think it could drop a bit before doing that so they place an order to buy at a lower price.

S: That's confusing.

P: Look at it this way. You know Nike and it is currently at $67 per share and you think it is going to hit triple digits. You don't want to pay the $67 so you place not a market order, but a limit order at $65. If the price drops to $65, your order will be executed.

S: That's a smart move, huh?

P: I don't agree with it. If you think the stock is going up significantly and it doesn't drop back before doing so, you'll be kicking yourself watching that stock go to $100 while your limit order remains at $65, most likely never to be executed.

S: I can't disagree with that. What's a stop-loss order?

P: This also is used in conjunction with other trading strategies beyond where you need to be at this time. An individual uses it is when they have a significant gain and want to protect it. Using the Nike illustration just discussed, let's say you did buy it at $67 and it goes to $100. You are happy with your $33 per share gain. You don't know what to do as you hope it keeps going up, but you are scared of it going down.

S: I could see that happening.

P: What you would do then is place a stop-loss order at, say, $96. That means if the price drops to $96, the investment company would sell Nike on your behalf.

S: I like this. I am guaranteed $96 per share?

P: You will be very close to that. The price may drop a little bit more before your trade is executed. It is only in the case of the entire market dropping dramatically that you could end up below $96 by $1 or more.

S: I could live with that. How about other types of stocks?

P: There are also *income stocks* which have above average dividend yields, but not major growth prospects. Many of these are utility companies.

S: What is a dividend yield?

P: A dividend yield is the total dividends to be paid in a year divided by the current share price. So, for instance, I'll use General Electric as an example. With a dividend of 24 cents per quarter, it paid an annual dividend of 96 cents. With its share price near $20, it was yielding 4.8 percent.

S: Wait a minute, so I was looking at 0.2 percent in a savings account and I can earn 4.8 percent from General Electric. I am putting all my money in General Electric; I'd be foolish not to.

P: Well, remember what just happened. They cut their dividend, for the second time in eight years, to 12 cents per share so your yield has just dropped to 2.7 percent ($0.48/$18 current price). A dropping stock price will mathematically increase your yield, but you certainly don't want yield increases that way.

S: I don't understand. Even if they cut the dividend, I am guaranteed 2.7 percent a year right?

P: You are only guaranteed the amount of any dividend that has been declared. If they eliminate the dividend, you get nothing.

S: Two things here, a company would be crazy to eliminate its dividend, and I would then sell my stock at $20 and then find another company.

P: Addressing your two things. Companies certainly don't like eliminating or cutting dividends, but sometimes they need the money for their operations. You probably have a lot of Mattel toys and they just recently eliminated their dividend. Secondly remember how I told you that your yield can increase because of a dropping stock price? Well if General Electric drops to $15, you now are taking a loss on the stock.

S: I bought it for $20 so don't I get the $20 back?

P: No, you get back whatever its value is at the time you sell it.

S: So, if I bought 100 shares by paying $2,000 and the stock drops to $15, I am only getting $1,500 back or $500 less. So my great quarterly dividend of $12 doesn't look too great at this time.

P: You have that right. Risk and reward.

S: Forget stocks, I want no risk whatsoever.

P: Your decision. The beauty of the markets is that each individual has their own risk and reward preference. You can do well but you need to do your homework or have a good financial advisor. Just so you know, it would have cost you $4.95 to buy the 100 shares and $4.95 to sell the 100 shares as a commission to the investment company.

S: Talk about adding insult to injury. I am getting charged to lose money.

P: You made the decision and those fees are dirt cheap compared to what they historically have been.

Now let's continue on, there are *cyclical stocks* which are stocks that follow the direction of the overall economy, but generally with more volatility than the market. What this means is if the economy is trending upward, these should move upward; if the economy is trending downward, they will move downward. Stocks in the automotive industry and heavy equipment manufacturers are known as cyclical stocks.

S: What do you mean by more volatility?

P: If the economy is moving upward and the stock market is moving upward, these stocks will outperform the market average but vice versa, the opposite holds if the economy and stock market move downward. Beta is a measure of the volatility of a stock and you would learn about this in your investments class.

Then there are *counter-cyclical or defensive stocks.*

S: Well these have to be stocks that move less than the market in general when it is moving up or down. What types of stocks are these?

P: Generally food companies, defense, and health care stocks have been noted as defensive stocks. However, remember that things change and food companies, particularly cereal companies, have been doing poorly recently as consumers look for healthier eating options.

There are also *speculative stocks*, some of which are *penny stocks* because of their low trading price. There is major uncertainty with respect to these companies due to negative developments usually. I would recommend you staying away from penny stocks for sure.

S: I often hear about large caps or small caps in the news so I thought you would be discussing those types of stocks. What is being discussed when commentators are talking about these?

P: They are referring to the market capitalization of a stock. The market capitalization is what the investing public says the company is worth; it is simply the number of shares owned by the current price of the stock. So, keeping it simple, if a company has 100 shares outstanding and its price is $10, it has a market capitalization of $1,000. The public says this company is worth $1,000.

S: How many different types of "caps" are there?

P: Good question. The number of caps has increased over the years. The general classifications are mega caps, large caps, mid caps, small caps, micro caps, and nano caps.

S: How is it determined what type of cap a company is?

P: Another good question, it is the market capitalization number. Mega caps have market capitalizations in excess of $200 billion while micro caps are less than $50 million. Every "cap" fits into a range and like the classification of stocks, they can move between categories over time.

The only thing I would tell you for sure is that many penny stocks are nano caps or micro caps so I would stay away from those with money that you need.

S: Why do they make up all these classifications?

P: Many mutual funds, which we will discuss later, will often focus specifically on stocks in one of the capitalization levels. So, for instance, a small cap fund will invest primarily in small cap stocks while certainly hoping they move up in classification.

S: What determines the price of a stock?

P: It is the most fundamental rule of supply and demand. As more people want to buy a stock, it moves up in price; as more people want to sell a stock, it moves down in price.

S: Now this is confusing, for every buyer there has to be a seller so they would have to balance. What if someone wants to sell and no one wants to buy?

P: This is where investment companies come into play. They are holding inventories of stock and help to keep a liquid market. As more people want to buy, some people are enticed to sell by a higher price or the investment company takes it out of its inventory. As more people want to sell, some people are enticed to buy by a lower price, or the investment company adds to its inventory. I would suggest you take a course in microeconomics which gets into supply and demand and many other factors involved in driving prices in many situations well beyond stocks. It will also provide you with a solid basis for analyzing common business decisions.

S: I have friends in macroeconomics. What is that?

P: It takes a bigger picture look at economics including, among many other things, what causes economies to expand and contract. I would suggest taking that also.

S: I only have 32 courses to take here.

P: Choose them wisely as there are many good courses to take and…if you are really ambitious and doing well, you can take more than 32.

S: So what do people look at when they figure out if they want to buy a stock?

P: Many different things. I will give you just a few and then remember some of the courses I suggested that you take.

Price/Earnings (PE) Ratio: The price of the stock divided by the earnings per share. Is the PE higher or lower than what it has been historically? Is the PE higher or lower than competitors?

Earnings Per Share: I'll give you the simple version here and not the accountant's version: Net income (i.e. profit)/total number of shares owned.

Payout Ratio: Dividends per share divided by earnings per share. Remember when I told you about General Electric cutting its dividend from 31 cents to 10 cents per share?

S: I do remember that.

P: Well back in December 2008, General Electric management "dismissed talk that the dividend might get be cut." (Glader, 2008) I had nursing and other majors in the personal finance class saying it was not sustainable based on the payout ratio. Not much later General Electric cut the dividend.

History has a way of repeating itself, the 2009 CEO recently retired and the new CEO said the dividend "is safe and reducing it won't be considered."(Gryta, 2017 July). His thinking then "evolved" and the dividend was cut from 24 cents to 12 cents.

Bottom line, if a company is paying out a large percentage of its earnings, it is not sustainable over a number of years.

Cash Flow from Operations: How much cash does a company generate from its basic operations or is it using cash in operations?

S: What do you think are the most important factors?

P: Many schools of thought here and I am often wrong more than I am right, but if a company can continually increase earnings and its cash generated from operations, everything else being equal, its stock price should be rising. The whole key is looking at the past, learning about the company and evaluating whether the trend can continue.

S: A lot of information to consider.

P: That is certainly true which is why I recommend mutual funds or dividend reinvestment plans (DRIPS) to first time investors.

S: What is a DRIP?

P: Remember we talked about dividends? With a DRIP, you don't take the dividend payment but you continually reinvest them in the company (which will be done automatically for you once you sign up). You can also make additional cash investments as you wish. I recommend setting up a regular payment if you are interested (this gets into dollar cost averaging which you can read about).

S: How do I get started in a DRIP?

P: Just search DRIPs on the internet and you'll find a lengthy list of companies. Many of them allow you to make your initial purchase with a pre-determined amount such as $250 as an example. To the right is an example of a DRIP statement. If you have the right stock, you can achieve slow but steady growth.

S: I see this company reduced its dividend. Is this just like General Electric?

P: Good observation but they actually did not reduce the dividend. Adient is an Irish company and the company that handles the DRIP plan started deducting a foreign withholding tax.

S: Is that deductible on a tax return?

P: You know my answer to that one.

S: The usual "take the tax course," so I will change topic. I have heard about preferred stocks, what is a preferred stock?

P: A preferred stock has preference over common stock with respect to dividends and in the event of the liquidation of the company.

S: What does all that mean?

P: Preferred shareholders will receive dividends (and usually at a set amount, they won't increase or decrease like those for common shareholders) before common shareholders can receive dividends. If the company is going out of business (unfortunately usually due to bankruptcy), the preferred shareholders have a right to assets before common shareholders). In reality, in most bankruptcies, there are no assets left for preferred or common shareholders.

Sign Off | Contact Us | Help

EQ
by Equiniti   **Shareowner Online**

| Account Overview | Transactions | Statements and Tax Forms | Alerts & Messages | My Account Settings |

| Security Overview | Transaction History | Sale History | Dividend and Sale Proceeds | Cost Basis |

Certificate/DRS Shares | Plan Shares |

Print, Download

Plan Share History

ADIENT PLC

Account Number: Security Type: **Ordinary Shares**

Cash Pending Investment ($):	100.00	Number of Shares Pending Sale/Withdrawal:	0.000		Dividend Reinvestment Status:	Full Dividend Reinvestment (RD)

Transaction Date	Transaction Type	Original Number of Shares	Gross Amount ($)	Tax Withholding ($)	Fees and Commission* ($)	Transaction Price/ Share ($)
Nov 17, 2017	Plan Distribution	0.246	18.93	0.00	.76	73.9396
Nov 10, 2017	Voluntary Contribution	1.230	100.00	0.00	4.06	78.0600
Aug 22, 2017	Plan Distribution	0.335	23.17	0.00	.95	66.3251
Aug 14, 2017	Voluntary Contribution	1.477	100.00	0.00	4.07	65.0100
May 22, 2017	Voluntary Contribution	1.332	100.00	0.00	4.07	72.0800
Apr 25, 2017	Plan Distribution	0.316	22.72	0.00	.93	69.0732
Feb 13, 2017	Voluntary Contribution	1.598	100.00	0.00	4.08	60.0630

Transaction fees paid by the Company may affect your taxes. If this applies, it will be reflected on your tax form(s)

To be frank, I would not recommend preferred stock for you until you are much older unless they are convertible into common. I'll leave that for your investments or accounting class. The majority of publicly traded companies do not offer preferred stock.

S: Once again, I am thinking about not touching stocks.

P: Your call, but a $10,000 investment years ago in Amazon when it went public in 1997 would have been worth almost $5 million at the end of October 2017 ("If You Had Invested," 2017) On the flip side, a $10,000 investment years ago in a bankrupt company would be worthless. Risk and reward.

S: Well, I'll buy Uber. I like their service.

P: You'll have to wait on that unless you have special connections. Uber is not yet a publicly traded company.

S: Why not?

P: Many reasons well beyond the scope of our discussion.

S: How many publicly traded companies are there?

P: As of November 2017, there were 3,671 publicly traded domestic companies on U.S. stock exchanges, about a 50 percent drop from 1996. (Thomas, 2017)

S: Why the significant drop?

P: A wide variety of reasons. Take the investments class as it is well beyond the scope of our discussion.

INVESTING BASICS – BONDS

STUDENT: I have a lot more questions about stocks.

PROFESSOR: I am glad to hear that as you should certainly have a lot more. Those questions will then lead to more. Never hesitate to ask them in your future classes; I unfortunately need to move on to bonds.

S: What is a bond?

P: Bonds are just formal borrowings by corporations, city, state and federal governments, government agencies, et cetera. They are different from stocks in that they are considered to be fixed income investments. This is certainly not always true but we will proceed on that basis.

S: How would I buy a bond?

P: Similar to a stock for all bonds except U.S. Treasury bonds. These can be bought via a website called U.S. Treasury Direct. They can also be bought through a bank or broker, but why pay any fees when you can buy direct? Other bonds would be bought through investment companies like stocks.

S: Why are bonds considered to be fixed income investments?

P: Because the income you receive is fixed over the life of the bond. Bonds, with the exception of zero coupon bonds, pay interest each year and then repay the face amount at maturity.

S: How often do they pay interest and what is the interest rate?

P: Most bonds pay interest two times per year at fixed intervals six months apart. The bond will have a face value, which is the maturity value (the amount you will receive at the due date of the bond) and a stated interest rate. The interest rate is paid based on the face value of the bond. Let me give you an example: A bond with a face value of $1,000 and a stated interest rate of 5 percent will pay $25 six months from the date on the bond and $25 on the date on the bond. (($1,000 * 5%)/2).

S: How many years will they pay this interest?

P: It depends on the length of the bond. Corporate bonds are generally 30 years long although some companies have longer bond terms. Some governments are going even longer than some of the longer corporate bonds. There are also shorter term bonds. Big picture, the longer the bond term, the more of an impact interest rates will have on the price of the bond, with everything else being equal.

S: This has to have something to do with the time value of money that we covered.

P: Well done.

S: So, if I understand, if I buy a bond of $1,000 paying 5 percent interest, I am going to pay $1,000 for the bond, get interest of $25 every six months for 30 years and then get my $1,000 back. I will need it long before then so no thanks to that.

P: You most likely be paying something other than $1,000. Bond prices are determined by supply and demand like stocks, but are quoted differently. For a $1,000 bond quoted at 97, you would pay $970 plus commission. For a $1,000 bond quoted at 103, you would pay $1,030 plus commission.

S: Just when I thought I had things figured out. Now I am definitely not buying bonds.

P: I'll agree with you on not buying bonds, but for different reasons. Most young people should be in stocks which historically have returned more than bonds. You have a longer period of time in which downturns can be offset by upturns. Bonds are for older people who don't want as much risk and need more of a fixed return.

S: Are you telling me that risk/return applies here also?

P: Risk/return applies in every area of personal finance we discuss. Remember when we discussed deductibles?

S: Right the higher the deductible, the lower the premium. Scary, but I am starting to see this now. With a higher deductible I am taking more risk and my return is my savings on my premium. What about the risk of fudging numbers on my tax return a bit?

P: Al Capone tried that and he died in jail, not because of murder convictions, but because of tax fraud. Besides, I know you would not do that.

Now back to bonds, the actual interest percent earned will differ from the face amount.

S: What??

P: We talked about a $1,000 bond with a 5 percent rate paying $50 per year right?

S: That is right. I can understand the simple math.

P: Well, as we discussed, it is most likely that the bond will sell for an amount greater than or less than $1,000, yet the interest payments received will still be $50 per year. If that is the case, the return each year will be greater than or less than 5 percent. For instance, if you bought the bond for $950, your annual return would be 5.3 percent.

S: Okay, mathematically I understand what is happening, but why would a bond with a face value of $1,000 sell for more or less than $1,000?

P: Two primary reasons: its credit rating and the current interest rates in the market.

S: Please explain its credit rating to me.

P: Sure, what is the grading system at Saint A's?

S: First of all, you mean Saint C's, and it is A, A-, B+, B, B-, C+, C, C-, D+, D, D-, and the always dreaded F.

P: Not to burst your bubble, but I already told you that Saint B's is really the correct name now. Well there are credit rating agencies for bonds. The three big ones are Standard & Poor (S&P), Moodys, and Fitch. They give grades to bonds based on the credit worthiness of the issuer (the company or government entity borrowing the money). For example, S&P gives ratings of AAA, AA, A, BBB, BB, B, CCC, CC, C, D, and NR. Moodys gives rating of Aa1, Aa2, A1, A2, A3, Baa1, Baa2, Baa2, Baa3, Ba1, Ba2, Ba3, B1, B2, B3, Caa1, Caa2, Caa3, Ca, and C.

S: Wow! What a grading system! I would like the AAA, AA and I could accept the BBB and BB at Saint A's as those would really help my GPA to throw even more initials in.

P: Right, but it is all relative. The bottom line is that two different companies issuing $1,000 bonds paying 5 percent will sell the bonds for different prices. I am going to ignore other interest rates in the market for this illustration. But given what I have told you right now, what bond (using the S&P ratings) would you want to buy?

S: Well I would want the AAA.

P: Correct for sure. Would you consider the AA?

S: Sure, but I won't pay as much for the AA.

P: How about the A?

S: Absolutely, but I won't pay as much as for the AA and certainly not as much as the AAA. I see your point now. To the extent you pay more, your effective return is lower, to the extent you pay less, your effective return is higher because you are always getting the same $50 each year.

P: You got it and believe it or not the value of the $1,000 30 years from now is also being considered, but we won't go into that.

S: That's a lot of grades those agencies are giving.

P: And that is only for long-term debt. Short-term debt has a maturity date less than a year and is given similar but different grades by the rating agencies.

S: Okay, let's go into the interest piece now.

P: Sure, have you ever heard a financial commentator or reporter say something like, "Bond prices rose today because interest rates dropped," or vice versa?

S: I actually have, but never gave it much thought.

P: Nor should you have, but it is a mathematical certainty.

S: Why is that?

P: The concept is the time value of money. Let me give you an example. Would you rather have $100 today or $105 a year from now?

S: This has to be a trick question.

P: Somewhat, the answer is that it depends.

S: I wish I could answer tests that way.

P: Unfortunately I see that sometimes, but let's continue on. It depends on what you can do with the money. If you can invest it and earn 4 percent, you would have $104 in a year so the answer would be to take the $105 a year from now. If you can invest it and earn 6 percent, you would have $106 a year from now, so the answer is to take the $100 now.

S: I see that mathematically, but what does that have to do with the value of bonds?

P: By inverting what we just did, we can assign a present value today to what we will receive in the future.

S: Now I am totally lost.

P: As I would expect you to be. The inversion is called a present value and the interest rate chosen is called a discount rate, so 4 percent one year from now carries a present value of 0.9615 (1/1.04) meaning a dollar a year from now is worth $0.9615 today. At 6 percent, it is a present value of 0.9434 (1/1.06) meaning a dollar a year from now is worth $0.9434 today. The higher the discount rate, the less the dollar a year from now is worth today.

S: Once again I see that mathematically, but how does this relate to bond pricing?

P: I'll appeal to your logic again and we'll assume the bonds I am discussing all have the same credit rating so we isolate the difference to the interest factor.

If interest rates are 6 percent in the market, would you pay $1,000 for a bond that pays an interest rate of 5 percent?

S: Why would I invest my $1,000 to earn 5 percent when I can earn 6 percent elsewhere with no additional risk?

P: Exactly, you are spot on. What do you think is going to happen?

S: Well you talked about something called the laws of supply and demand. If no one is demanding the 5 percent bond, its price has to drop.

P: And we have discussed the real return (or yield) before. What happens as the price drops?

S: Well, as the price drops, the yield increases. Don't tell me that the price is going to drop to where the bond is yielding 6 percent.

P: Exactly, and now tell me what happens if interest rates in the market are 4 percent.

S: Just the opposite, if people can only earn 4 percent elsewhere, the price of the bond paying 5 percent will be bid up until it is yielding 4 percent. You are correct, it is mathematically true.

P: Absolutely, in the "real" world, there are two components for which present values are calculated to determine the price of the bond. Present values are computed for the income stream over the life of the bond, and also a present value is computed for the maturity value of the bond.

There are many websites that can do these calculations so just do a search some day and you'll be pleasantly surprised by the sheer number of financial websites.

S: I actually understand the mathematical calculations of bonds. What else can you tell me about bonds?

P: Again, we'll just cover the basics. There are secured and unsecured bonds. Secured bonds have a claim on some of the assets of the company in the event of financial difficulties. Unsecured bonds, which are also referred to as debenture bonds, do not have a claim on any specific assets.

S: Who comes first in the event of financial difficulties of a company?

P: It gets quite complicated for sure. For purposes of the investments that we have covered, the order is secured creditors, unsecured creditors, preferred shareholders, common shareholders.

S: You told me that preferred shareholders and common shareholders generally will get nothing in the case of a bankruptcy. What about secured and unsecured creditors?

P: Secured creditors will probably get some money back but, in most cases, just a portion of their investment and the percentage can vary significantly between bankruptcies. Unsecured creditors, if they get anything, will receive a much smaller percentage than secured creditors and we have already discussed the likely outcome for stockholders.

S: What about a company that comes out of bankruptcy? I have read about that happening.

P: That is always the hope when bankruptcy is entered, as employee jobs and business relationships are on the line. One of the reasons a company is able to come out of bankruptcy is because it has been able to "shed" its debt so it generally does not change the situation for all the parties just discussed. They absorb their losses and move on.

S: Any other types of bonds?

P: Many including convertible, callable, redeemable, et cetera. Those are well beyond what I want to cover with you though.

S: It will get covered in an investments course though right? How about if the stock price is doing well, does the value of my bond increase?

P: Only if it is a convertible bond which has the right to be exchanged for common shares. Again, I'll leave that for an investment class.

S: I hear about tax-exempt bonds. Are most bonds tax-exempt?

P: Tax-exempt bonds are generally issued by government entities. It is a way to allow cities and towns and other agencies to borrow at a lower interest rate and save money.

S: I don't understand, why are interest rates lower on tax-exempt bonds?

P: You're getting pretty good with figuring things out mathematically, let's try that approach. Remember when we talked about the marginal tax rate long ago when we talked about taxes?

S: I do. It is the rate that you pay on each additional dollar earned.

P: Excellent! And what did I say your marginal tax rate would most likely be?

S: I think I remember either 12 percent or 22 percent.

P: Well done again. Now we won't worry about state taxes now, just federal taxes. State tax rates vary widely; the key point is to understand the concept and whatever state you end up living in, you can make the necessary adjustments to the calculation.

Let's assume you are in the 12 percent tax bracket and you have a choice of investing in a corporate bond paying 7.5 percent, or a tax-exempt bond paying 6 percent. From a purely financial standpoint, which do you invest in?

S: You're kidding me right? I have absolutely no idea.

P: I'll respectfully disagree with you. Just take a minute and think it through.

S: Okay, I'll use simple numbers like you always do.

P: Wise move, if you can understand it with simple numbers, what difference does adding a lot of zeroes in the equation matter?

S: So if I have a $100 bond paying 7.5 percent interest or $7.50, and I am in a 12 percent tax bracket, I will pay 90 cents in federal taxes and have $6.60 left after taxes. If I buy a tax-exempt bond, I pay no federal taxes and have $6 so, everything else being equal, the corporate bond is the better buy for me. But how can they sell tax-exempt bonds if corporate bonds are always a better buy?

P: You tell me. Let's assume now that you are in the 22 percent tax bracket and everything else is the same. Which one is your better investment?

S: Well, let's see, I am still getting $7.50 and if I am in the 22 percent bracket, I will pay $1.65 in taxes and have $5.85 left after taxes. With the tax-exempt bond, I will get the same $6, so now I have a different answer. You told me marginal tax rates mattered but I had no idea how.

P: Now you understand. Ironically, investments in federal bonds and treasury bills (short-term investments in government securities) are not tax exempt at the federal level but are at the state level.

S: More tax talk? I know where this is heading. "Take a tax class."

P: Better you say it than me!

INVESTING BASICS – MUTUAL FUNDS

STUDENT: Let's discuss mutual funds now. I hear a lot about them but don't know much about how they work, and I hear about index funds and exchange traded funds and have no idea about them at all.

PROFESSOR: You're not alone. We'll discuss mutual funds in general and then we can briefly discuss index funds and exchange traded funds. First thing is a bit of trivia: As of December 31, 2016, there were 9,511 different mutual funds ("Mutual Funds," n.d.)with net assets of $16.34 trillion. ("Total Net Assets," n.d.) At that date, approximately 43.6 percent of U.S. households were invested in a mutual fund. If I look at Fidelity's website now, they say there are over 10,000 mutual funds so either way, there are many.

S: Did you say trillions? And what are "net" assets?

P: Yes, trillions and net assets are simply assets-liabilities.

S: This has something to do with accounting right?

P: Absolutely, if you are looking at companies, why not understand some of what is in their financial statements? Even more, you will generally find worthwhile information in the footnotes that will help you to better understand the financial statements.

S: Got it, got it. So explain the key information to me.

P: Any guess as to how I am going to explain the basics of a mutual fund to you?

S: Yes, using simple numbers.

P: Let's get started then. Firstly, a mutual fund takes money entrusted to it by many investors and looks to invest it wisely and in accordance with the fund's stated objectives. I'll discuss the many different types of mutual funds later. Mutual funds are managed by investment managers, most of whom are employed by the investment companies which we have previously discussed.

S: So if I understand you correctly, if I invest in a mutual fund, say with Fidelity, I am throwing my money into a pot with a lot of other people that I don't know?

P: Good way of looking at it. You would have hopefully done your "due diligence" and selected the proper type of fund or listened to a good investment advisor.

S: You've managed to go quite a while without saying due diligence.

P: I know, it was quite overdue, no pun intended wise guy.

Let's say you selected a stock fund and—again keeping it simple—at the end of the day, it has two investments: Company A, which has a value of $100, and Company B, which has a value of $75. It has other assets of $10 and liabilities of $15 so it has net assets at the end of the day of $170 ($100 + $75 + $10 - $15). It has 50 shares outstanding thus it has a net asset value (NAV) of $3.40 per share.($170 divided by 50). For most mutual funds, NAV is the key because when you place an order it is executed at the NAV at 4 p.m. (EST). that day. . If you place the order at 4 p.m. or later, it is executed at the NAV at 4 p.m. the following day.

S: I have it so far. So say the NAV at the end of the day was $3.40 and I decide to buy the next day, what happens? Let's say I invest $50.

P: Well, let's say at the end of the next day, Company A had a value of $110, Company B had a value of $80, other assets remained the same at $10, and liabilities increased to $17. What is the NAV of the company at that time?

S: Well, it would be $110 + $80 + $10 - $17 = $183. I would then divide the $183 by the 50 shares and get a NAV of $3.66. Seems to make sense as Companies A and B had good increases in value.

P: Right, now your $50 is divided by $3.66 and you now own 13.661202 shares.

S: That's a funny number.

P: It happens a lot with DRIPs and other investments if you remember that DRIP statement I showed you. The 0.661202 is considered to be a fractional share. More importantly, what is the NAV after your investment?

S: Well, it has to go down because the $183 is now divided by the 63.661202 shares outstanding, so it is $2.87. Wow, I have lost money already and haven't done a thing.

P: Think logically, do you think an investment would cause NAV to decrease?

S: Logically no, but mathematically it is.

P: Well did your $50 disappear into thin area within the mutual fund?

S: Aah...I have to think about this one...I'm struggling with this one.

P: What does the $50 you put into the mutual fund become?

S: Based on what was there before, it increases other assets so let's see, we now have ($183 + $50)/63.661202 = $3.66. Son of a b—...gun.

P: Good job catching yourself. Save your swearing for the golf course when you miss those short putts.

S: But what if I wanted to buy a specific number of shares? Am I able to do that and how would that work?

P: Absolutely, you can do that. What is it going to cost you to buy 10 shares in the illustration we have used?

S: Well, the NAV at 4 p.m. after I placed the order was $3.66, so it will cost me $36.60. But how do I know that I need to transfer exactly $36.60 to them?

P: You're not transferring that to them. Remember you already have an account balance with them so they are merely reducing your cash balance. The one thing you need to do is to make sure you estimate approximately how much your purchase will cost you and make sure you have more than enough funds to cover it. That way if the NAV increases significantly due to a good market day, you can still make your purchase.

S: Got it. Is there a commission when you buy a mutual fund?

P: Excellent question. It depends on whether it is a load fund which charges commissions or a no load fund which does not charge commissions. These are when you buy; there are also back load funds which is a fancy name for a commission when you sell. The key for you is to know what type of fund you are buying before you buy.

S: Let's run through how the calculation would work.

P: Certainly, we'll look at a front end load (i.e. when you buy). Understand this and you can easily do the same for a back end load fund. We'll use the same numbers we have been using for consistency.

If you were investing your $50 and the load was 3 percent, they would deduct $1.50 and you would now be investing $48.50, so you would get 13.251366 shares (or 3 percent less than you previously got). The rest of the math remains the same.

S: I am understanding this. How much do loads run and which are better, load funds or no load funds?

P: Great questions, the maximum allowable load is 8.5 percent (Ouch!); the average seems to run around 5 percent. The second question you posed is the subject of great debate. You can find academic papers claiming load funds perform better, and you can find academic papers claiming no load funds pay better.

S: Which do you prefer, being as cheap as you say? You must prefer no load funds.

P: Surprisingly, I have bought load funds, as I liked the performance of specific funds. I've never paid more than 3 percent and I don't buy a lot of mutual funds. I have been lucky, I think, to achieve through my investments one of the benefits of mutual funds.

S: Which is?

P: Diversification.

S: Diversification meaning you diversify your investments? By owning different investments, if one or more go down, it can hopefully be offset by one or more going up?

P: Exactly. With all the different investments owned by the fund, they are achieving diversification within their stated investment objective.

S: How do I know what my mutual fund's investment objective is and what they own?

P: Hopefully, you will know the objective and that it is in line with yours before you buy the fund. This is contained in a prospectus which breaks down their holdings into easily followed groupings. It will also show the top 5 investments among other information. After you buy the stock, you will get a semi-annual (every six months) which shows the investment mix at the report date.

S: So what are the different types of mutual funds?

P: First we'll talk about basic open-end funds. There are different names that are used but they cover the same basics. I will illustrate one such groupings. For instance, at AmericanFunds.com, they list the types as:

Growth Funds – Looking for growth stocks

Growth and Income Funds – Growth stocks which also pay dividends

Equity-Income Funds – Focusing on dividend paying stocks

Balanced Funds – Seeks a balance between stocks, bonds, and cash investments

Bond Funds – You know what this is focusing on

Cash Equivalent Funds – Investing in short-term money market funds and other short-term investments

Target Date Funds – A mix of stocks, bonds, and cash depending on a person's expected retirement period. For instance, through our retirement plan, I have been put in the 2020 plan (although I am looking at leaving in 2040 at the earliest) whereas you would most likely be put in the 2060 plan. Your plan would have a much larger percentage invested in stocks than mine.

S: Because at a younger age, I have a much better chance of recovering from a significant reduction in the market.

P: Excellent and lastly, per the American.com website, there are portfolio series funds which are really mutual funds investing in other mutual funds.

S: That happens?

P: Yes, diversification on steroids. My wise remark does not mean it is bad. Do you remember when we talked about market capitalization?

S: Yes I do. The market capitalization of a company is the number of shares outstanding times the price of the stock. It is what the public thinks the company is worth.

P: Excellent again and guess what? There are large-cap funds, mid-cap funds, small-cap funds; there are sector (companies within a specific industry) funds; there are social investing funds. Basically, you think about how you would like your money invested and you will find a fund to meet your expectations on how your money is invested. Notice I did not say goals with respect to the results.

S: I did notice that. So there are no guarantees with respect to mutual funds despite the diversification achieved.

P: None whatsoever. Probably the only sure thing is short-term money market funds.

S: And, of course, the expected return is low on these? Risk versus reward again.

P: Absolutely, if you only need to preserve and not grow your money significantly, that is the investment for you. You won't have major income, but your downside is very limited, if not non-existent.

S: When would I want to be in short-term money market funds?

P: Everyone has a different opinion, but I would say before you need money for a major expenditure. For instance, if you are saving for a down payment for a house, you probably want less exposure to the stock market. If your children are going to college in 2 – 4 years, you'd hate to have a significant market downturn reduce that money. If you have a child getting married in another year, you would not want all your money in the market.

Do you remember I told you about the 9.65% effective annual return on the S&P 500 including reinvested dividends over a 90 year period?

S: I certainly do, that is quite impressive.

P: Yes it is, but always bear in mind that there were negative returns in 24 years including a losing streak of four years and two losing streaks of 3 years.

Similar to target date funds, as you age the percentage of stocks in your portfolio (investments) should be decreasing and the percentage in fixed income funds, including money market funds, should be increasing.

S: That makes sense. What is an index fund?

P: An index fund looks to track or match the performance of some pre-determined stock index like the S&P 500, the Russell 2000, or the Wilshire 5000. The number refers to the number of stocks included in the index (although the Wilshire only has about 3,500 due to the shrinking number of U.S. stocks). If the index is increasing significantly in value, your NAV should be also and, of course, if the index is declining, your NAV should be declining.

S: What is the advantage of investing in an index fund?

P: Index funds come with lower expense ratios since they are passively managed. I need to explain two things here to you that we have not discussed. First, each mutual fund will report an expense ratio which is its total expenses/total net assets.

S: More math?

P: Throughout finance, but again think logically. If Mutual Fund A has an expense ratio of 1.5 percent and Mutual Fund B has an expense ratio of 0.3 percent what is true?

S: Well logically, for Mutual Fund A to be a better investment than Mutual Fund B, A's returns have to be at least 1.2 percent greater than B's returns.

P: Precisely.

S: So lower expense ratio mutual funds are always better.

P: There are no certainties in the investment world, you know that by now. The second new concept I discussed is why the expense ratio is lower. A passively managed investment is not actively moving in and out of stocks. If you are just trying to replicate the

S&P 500, there are only 500 possible stocks you can own and you are trying to keep the ratio consistent with the index. Actively managed funds incur more expenses moving in and out of investments and having more research costs.

S: With all these potential costs, how do I find out what a mutual fund will cost me?

P: Without overly complicating this, there are three common types of mutual fund share classes: A, B, and C (there can be others). Class A shares generally charge a load (commission) at the time of purchase. Class B shares do not charge a load at the time of purchase, but the annual expenses are higher and you will most likely pay a load at time of sale. The load generally decreases over time and your shares could convert into Class A shares. Class C shares do not charge a load but generally have higher expenses over time.

S: Clear as mud to me.

P: It was that way to me also when I was younger. That said, the Financial Industry Regulatory Authority (FINRA) has an excellent fund analyzer program that will lay out the loads, expenses, historical returns, et cetera for any fund you want to consider. Have a look at it when you have a chance.

S: I will do that and, despite my comment, I do have the basic concepts. How about an exchange traded fund?

P: An exchange traded fund is an index fund but whose shares are bought and sold throughout the day at the price existing at that time, not at a price established at 4 p.m. You would have quotes on it similar to what you have on a stock, and the value should be always very close to the NAV. If not, it is an arbitrage opportunity which is well beyond the scope of our discussion.

S: Any other types of funds I should be aware of?

P: Well the type of fund which we discussed using numbers is an open-end fund, which means anyone can buy shares at any time. There is not a limit to the number of shares. A closed-end fund will have only a fixed number of shares and, like an exchange traded fund, trades throughout the day. Unlike an exchange traded fund, its shares can trade at a significant difference from NAV. The price can be higher than NAV which means it is trading at a premium or lower than NAV, which means it is trading at a discount.

S: Why would the price differ from the NAV?

P: You tell me based on what we have discussed.

S: Supply and demand. Supply, the number of shares is fixed so weak demand reduces the price, and strong demand increases the price. Give me some numerical examples so I make sure I understand this.

P: Sure, if the NAV is $15 and the shares are selling for $16.50, the shares are trading at a premium; if the NAV is $15 and the shares are selling for $13.50, the shares are trading at a discount.

S: I am going to make a fortune. If the NAV is $15 and the shares are selling for $13.50, I'll take loans and buy as much as I can and make $1.50 per share because the price will eventually get to $15.

P: What if the market has a bad run and the NAV drops to $13? Do you like your chances now?

S: No, you don't understand. I will buy at $13.50 and sell at $15 immediately.

P: Well who is going to buy it from you at $15 when they can buy it in the market at $13.50?

S: I see, my millions just went up in smoke. It seems everything we discussed has some tax angle. What's the catch with mutual funds?

P: There is something unique with respect to mutual funds. Mutual funds distribute dividends generally on a quarterly basis and capital gains just before year end. Similar to stocks and bonds, you have a cost basis (the actual purchase cost including commissions) and a sales proceeds amount (the actual sales value minus commissions). If your sales proceeds exceed your cost basis when you sell some shares, you have a capital gain. Likewise, if your sales proceeds are less than your cost basis, you have a capital loss.

S: Oh! So these are those capital gains that I always hear being discussed on the news as tax rates are being discussed.

P: Partially, the key is that long term capital gains (LTCG) pay taxes at a lower tax rate than short term capital gains (STCG).

S: How low?

P: Well remembering marginal tax rates, there is a 12 percent bracket, a 22 percent bracket, and then brackets above 22 percent. Let's focus on the 12 percent tax rate. If you are in the 12 percent bracket, you owe no taxes on your LTCGs. If you are in the 22 percent bracket, you will be taxed at 15 percent on your LTCGs. Just for full disclosure, high income taxpayers will have a maximum marginal rate of 23.8 percent on LTCGs, but that explanation is better given elsewhere.

S: How do you determine if it is LTCG or STCG?

P: You are asking all the right questions. LTCG is for shares you have owned more than 12 months. STCGs are for shares you have owned for 12 months or less.

S: So, if I am in the 12 percent bracket and have LTCGs of $100,000, I will owe no taxes on that $100,000?

P: No, some of your LTCG would be taxed at zero, but some would be subject to the preferential LTCG rate of 15 percent as your LTCGs have pushed your income into the 22 percent bracket.

S: Tax course?

P: Always a recommendation. The tax calculation is not bad as the *Internal Revenue Service* (IRS) provides a helpful schedule to allow you to calculate your tax liability.

S: I'm getting tired of mutual funds, but you mentioned that there was a unique tax aspect to mutual funds and then what you just explained with respect to LTCGs and STCGs, you said the same applies to stocks and bonds.

P: You listen well. I got side-tracked because I wanted to cover LTCGs. I was talking about mutual funds distributing dividends on a quarterly basis. These are taxable to you the year distributed. Mutual funds are also required to distribute realized capital gains on an annual basis. This is after reducing them for any realized capital losses.

S: What is a realized capital gain?

P: The mutual fund had a stock for which it paid $10. If it is sold for $15, it is a realized gain. If it is not sold and the value at the end of the year is $15, it is an unrealized gain. Realized gains and losses is where you have actually made the sale.

Now with mutual funds being required to distribute realized capital gains, you will have reportable capital gains on your tax return for the year distributed. If you buy a mutual fund near year end and it then has a capital gain distribution, you have taxable income.

S: Sorry, but I am at the "Huh?" stage again.

P: And I don't blame you again. Let's take an extreme example. Say you buy a mutual fund for $12 per share and in the next couple of weeks they have a capital gain distribution of $1 per share. Let's say there were absolutely no changes in net assets during the period between when you bought the stock and when the capital gains were distributed, what was the NAV just prior to the distribution?

S: Well, it would be $12 per share.

P: Correct and after they give you and every other shareholder $1 per share.

S: Well, again mathematically, it now has to be $11 per share. So, you are saying my investment is worth $1 per share less. I am no wealthier and I am effectively paying taxes on the $1 that they returned to me.

P: You are spot on.

S: How can I be taxed when I am in the same position as before?

P: Unfortunately those are the rules and trying to do it any other way would be even more confusing.

S: But I have been taxed on my own money, it has to even out somewhere.

P: I love to see you thinking logically. It does. Again, dealing with an extreme example to illustrate the point, assume again there has been no change in NAV and you sell the stock.

S: Right, and I get $11 per share.

P: So how much have you gotten in total distributions?

S: The $1 dividend and the $11 from selling the share, so I have my $12 back, but I still owe taxes at my marginal rate on the dividend. So because I am paying taxes on my own money, I have been penalized.

P: No, where it evens out is that you have a basis (cost) of $12 in your share and you sold it for $11 so you have a $1 STCL, which offsets your dollar of dividend income.

S: This sure is confusing.

P: Yes, it is and I know you are sick of hearing my recommendation, but there are many tax areas where, if you know the tax consequences before making the decision, you can put yourself in better position. As I have said before, taxes should not drive decisions but their impact should be known in advance.

S: My head is spinning. Anything else?

P: Although I think we have hit information overload, I'll tell you two more things.

S: Did you used to be a torturer?

P: Well…Firstly, qualified dividends receive a preferential tax rate identical to LTCGs so they are good.

S: What is a qualified dividend?

P: It would be pure torture if I got into those rules but suffice it to say, your brokerage company or wherever you have invested your money will tell you what is qualified and what is not. For most investors, the great majority if not all of their dividends are qualified.

S: And secondly?

P: I strongly recommend you reinvest all your mutual fund dividends and capital gains just like I recommended you reinvest all the dividends for your stocks. If they are kept with the brokerage or custodian company, it will reinvest them on your behalf and your basis (cost) will be available for you from that company for tax computation purposes when you sell them.

S: And what if I bought them directly from the company as discussed during the initial conversation about DRIP plans?

P: That's when you set up an Excel spreadsheet and keep track of your basis on your own. As long as you save each year end statement, you'll be fine and I'll show you a way to set up the spreadsheet if you wish.

S: I'm going to the pub. Why so much time on mutual funds?

P: Well, I can't say as I blame you for going to the pub, and I will answer the final question. Most people will do their investing through mutual funds so the more you know, the better off you will be.

MEDICAL INSURANCE

STUDENT: Why do I need to think about medical insurance? I have always been in good health, I keep myself in good shape, and I have never had a serious accident.

PROFESSOR: Just because you are discussing those factors means you understand the risks that medical insurance is covering. Believe me, you don't want to break a leg and not have medical insurance.

S: Well I heard that I can stay on my parents' plan through age 26 so why are we even talking about this?

P: You can stay on your parents' plan until you turn age 26, as long as they have elected to cover you. Hopefully you'll be reimbursing them for the significant additional costs they are incurring.

S: I'll figure that out later. Do you mean once I am 26, I am no longer covered under their plan?

P: That is correct although some plans will allow you to stay through the end of the year in which you turn 26. You want to make sure you know the rules sooner rather than later. It is always easier to adjust to changes that may occur rather than try to learn all the facts when many things are happening.

Hopefully, you'll find an employer offering a plan equal to or superior than your parents' plan; if not you can stay on your parents' plan until the deadline.

S: So what do I need to know about health care?

P: As we have done with all the topics covered, I am just going to discuss the basics with you. Health care is very fluid so if you understand the basics and have someone's brain to pick with respect to choices, that is your ideal scenario. Fortunately, I have always had good plans via my employers so, with the exception of a 15 month period, have not had to worry about picking it up on my own.

S: Well let's get started.

P: Just so you understand, health care has many acronyms so I will be using and explaining quite a few.

S: More acronyms than we have seen already in other topics?

P: Far more!

Let's review some basics though that are common to most plans. What do you think a premium is?

S: Well in auto and homeowners insurance a premium is what was paid for the insurance coverage. So there must be premiums with a health insurance policy.

P: Exactly, and if you are on a plan through your employer, the premiums are normally deducted each payroll cycle.

S: What are the chances of my having insurance via my employer?

P: Let me tell you first that the 2016 Census Bureau Report on health insurance indicated that approximately 61 percent of insured people receive their insurance through an employer plan; the next largest groups of insured are Medicaid and Medicare. (Barnet and Berchik, 2017)

I did read an article which stated that 96 percent of large employers offered health insurance plans versus 29.4 percent of small employers offering such plans. (King, 2017)

S: Bottom-line, if I work for a large employer, I will probably have health care insurance offered?

P: You are getting good at cutting to the chase.

S: If I choose to work for a small employer, I have about a 30 percent chance of being offered health insurance?

P: An excellent question to ask after you have been offered the job. Also, learn the specifics about the plan as there can be significant differences between them.

S: Okay, let's get to the acronyms you have been mentioning.

P: Yes, but let's just review a few terms first. Do you remember what a deductible is?

S: Yes, that is the amount that you are responsible for before insurance kicks in to cover the balance.

P: Very good. Now in health care coverage, there are co-pays and co-insurance. A co-pay is what you are responsible each visit or each time you get a prescription. For instance, a co-pay for an

HMO (to be discussed) may be $25. Co-insurance means you are paying a portion of the cost. For example, you may have co-insurance of 20 percent, meaning you are paying 20 percent of the cost.

S: Either way, I have some out-of-pocket costs.

P: That is correct. Now for the acronyms...first is what I already mentioned, an HMO which is a health maintenance organization. An HMO provides you with a network of healthcare providers and facilities You have a primary care physician who will direct you to specialists if necessary. The key with the HMO is that your primary care physician will only refer you to specialists within the HMO network. If you go to someone outside of that specific network, generally you have to pay the full bill yourself. However there are exceptions that I will discuss.

S: Knowing that healthcare costs are high, that's enough incentive for me to go to a specialist within the network.

P: It certainly is, but always know that in case of an emergency, you can go to an out of network provider however, if they bill at a higher rate than your HMO rate, you may have to pay the difference. Also, if they don't have a specialist in the network for a medical situation, you will be able to go out of network. To cite a couple of examples, medical procedures such as a solid organ transplant or, if you have children, pediatric back surgery may require an out of network specialist.

S: Do you recommend that in an emergency, I wait to get to an HMO hospital?

P: Not in any way, shape, or form. Go to the most readily available location and get treated.

Now there are co-pays or co-insurance with HMOs and they do count towards reaching the deductible.

S: Got it. I have the gist of an HMO. With respect to co-pays or co-insurance though, what is better for me?

P: Certainly a co-pay. That is all that you are required to pay. With co-insurance, you are paying a percentage so you are certainly hoping for a low bill, but you've heard enough about medical bills.

S: Co-pay for sure! What other acronyms do you have for me?

P: There are PPOs or preferred provider organizations.

S: And the difference between an HMO and a PPO is?

P: Another excellent question and just so you know, the differences between all the acronyms seem to be lessening so I am speaking in generalities. With a PPO you have a bit more freedom than an HMO. You will have a list of all doctors, including specialists, who are in the PPO network. You'll have a primary care physician, but you don't need a referral to see a specialist if the specialist is a member of the network.

S: What if I have heard about an excellent specialist for a specific problem that I have, but that specialist is not part of the network?

P: You can certainly use this specialist, but you will pay more than if you were to see an in-network specialist.

S: How much more?

P: That can vary widely. You can always ask these questions of your PPO well in advance. Remember that if you need a specialist for a procedure, for which they do not have a specialist in the PPO network, your expenses will most likely be covered as if the specialist were a member of the network.

S: Does a PPO have deductibles, co-pays, or co-insurance?

P: You are getting great at asking the right questions. Yes, a PPO certainly does.

S: Now we are back to the co-pay versus co-insurance question and I am certainly searching for the co-pay option. I am ready for another acronym.

P: Glad to see you are getting into the spirit of this. The next is an EPO or an exclusive provider organization. This provides you with more freedom than an HMO as you do not have to have your primary care doctor refer you to a specialist. The downside is that if you see an out of network specialist, you will have to pay for the full cost. Please note however that in all plans, emergencies are covered subject to the cost differential previously discussed. Additionally, the same rules apply if you need a specialist that the EPO cannot provide.

S: Okay, so it is more restrictive than a PPO. Can I guess that because it is more restrictive and probably has a smaller number of providers, the premium is lower than a PPO?

P: See, the logic in other areas applies to most areas involving finances. Nice job.

S: Deductibles, co-pays, or co-insurance with an EPO?

P: Plan specific of course. Some EPOs may have a deductible, most likely there is a co-pay or co-insurance, and remember the major point of picking up the full cost if you go out of network other than for an emergency or to a specialist when they have a similar specialist in network.

S: Understood. What other plans are there?

P: A POS or point of service plan is a hybrid of the HMO and PPO. You have more freedom than an HMO, but you will still have a primary care physician who will refer you to specialists. Similar to other plans, you will pay more if you go out of network.

S: Let me guess, there are deductibles, co-pay, or co-insurance. Got it. And next?

P: Next up is the catastrophic plan which is available to you since you are under 30.

S: Not sure I like the sound of this one!

P: Well, it is designed so that you have relatively low cost health insurance, however it uses the risk/reward trade-off consistent with many other areas of personal finance we have discussed. Namely, as a trade-off for the lower cost, you have a significantly higher deductible.

S: Just how high are you talking?

P: First some of the additional benefits. You will have three primary care visits before the deductible applies and you have free preventive care even if you have not met the deductible. You can see any doctor in the network and plans have different rules on specialists.

S: And of course, premiums, deductibles…which I am still waiting to hear about, co-pays or co-insurance.

P: You are correct on premiums and deductibles, but there are no co-pays or co-insurance with a catastrophic plan. Now for the deductible that you have been so anxious to hear about; in 2017 it was $7,150 for an individual and $14,300 for a family. ("Understanding Health," n.d.)

S: Ouch!

P: Well, if you are not saying ouch much over the course of a year, it is not a bad plan for you. Hopefully, you suffer no major injuries. If your mindset is that you are 26 and don't need health insurance, then the catastrophic plan is a viable alternative for you. The deductible would be painful if you suffer a major injury, but much better than having no coverage at all.

S: Boy, I was okay with the risk/reward trade-off everywhere else but this is getting serious now.

P: All the more reason to know all the options available to you so you make the most informed choice. Just one other thing of which you need to be aware. If you have an injury and you have a catastrophic plan, the insurer has negotiated rates for various procedures. In short, the charges are going to be lower if you are a member of a plan than if you are an individual walking in off the street and not in a plan.

S: All these options, weighing all the choices and numbers certainly makes medical insurance a tough choice.

P: I don't disagree. Now for some more acronyms there are HDHPs with or without a HSA.

S: You're enjoying laying all this on me too much.

P: Yes I am, but it is the nature of the beast. A HDHP is a high deductible health plan and a HSA is a health savings account. With a HDHP, you may have a HMO, PPO, EPO, or POS. As the name says, you will have a higher deductible with no co-pays or co-insurance. You may have a HSA, which is tax deductible.

S: For adjusted gross income or after adjusted gross income?

P: Now I am really impressed that you are remembering the importance of that. It is for AGI. You can only have a HSA if you are in a HDHP.

S: So in exchange for a lower premium, what sort of a deductible are we talking about?

P: Excellent question once again. It is plan specific and in 2017 can range from $1,300 to $6,550 for an individual, and the range is $2,600 to $13,300 for a family.

S: Co-pays or co-insurance?

P: Very plan specific

S: And how much can I put into a HSA?

P: In 2017, the limits were $3,400 for an individual and $6,750 for a family.

S: What else is there?

P: Sorry, but I am all out of acronyms for now.

S: Well my head is certainly spinning.

P: Yes, but you were asking the right questions. You know enough to ask the right questions when alternatives are put in front of you.

S: Anything else?

P: Keep good track of your medical expenses. Set up an Excel spreadsheet for each year and have a file for all your receipts. Normally, the provider bills the insurance company and the insurance company bills you for your share after figuring it out. With co-pays or co-insurances, you may well be paying these up front. If you go out of network and it is covered, you generally pay the provider directly and then seek reimbursement.

Big picture, track your expenses carefully as you will know when you hit the deductible threshold, and it may before the insurer realizes it. That said, an employer's benefit plan and a flexible spending account (FSA)—to be discussed—will make the paperwork much easier for you

S: You had to throw that last acronym in there, and there seems to be paperwork everywhere.

P: There always will be in many financial areas, but it is getting better.

S: Do you always choose the lowest cost plan when you have choices?

P: No, when my kids were young, we were lucky we had two good choices and one was lower cost than the other. The issue though was that I was living 50 miles from where I worked and the higher cost network had more providers in our area than the lower cost one, which had more near my place of employment. So check out the provider network and figure out which works best for you.

S: What about the Affordable Care Act plans?

P: I can only tell you the basics of these.

The four plans and the approximate coverages are bronze (approximately 60 percent coverage), silver (approximately 70 percent coverage), gold (approximately 80 percent coverage), and platinum (approximately 90 percent coverage). (Wilson, 2016) I have also listed these from least costly to most costly.

Bronze plans have a $6,000 deductible for medical expenses and $500 for prescription drugs.

Silver plans have a $2,250 deductible for medical expenses and $250 for prescription drugs.

Gold and platinum plans have small deductibles.

There are different payment levels for different medical services provided. If you want to see specifics, I found a good spot to be www.medicoverage.com/health-insurance. Seeing the table there reminded me of something I had forgotten to mention to you.

S: There is more?

P: This is a "benefit" to you. It is referred to as a "stop loss" provision which means you have a maximum dollar amount that you can spend each year. After you hit the maximum, 100 percent of all costs are covered no matter what the co-pay or co-insurance provisions say.

S: Must be pretty high.

P: Once again, you are understanding the relationships. It varies by plan but, for instance for those Affordable Care Act plans, for the gold plan it is $6,500 for an individual and $13,000 for a family. The respective numbers for the platinum plan are $4,000 and $8,000.

One other factor is only the silver plan qualifies for cost sharing subsidies whereby you only pay a portion of the cost. The subsidy is based on income levels and is well beyond the scope of what we are covering.

S: What are the costs?

P: Dependent on many factors including your income and the number of members in your household to be covered. Search ACA plans and you will find your answer with some work as it is very individual specific including the city and state in which you live. Bottom line is if you are single and make less than $47,520, you are eligible for some subsidy, but the closer to $47,520 you make, the lower the subsidy.

S: Can we review a representative plan?

P: I'll do you one better. In a little bit, I'll review the benefits package offered at Saint Anselm of which one component is health insurance.

S: What are we talking about next?

P: Disability insurance.

S: Another pleasant topic.

P: I appreciate your cynicism, but it is important that you understand this. Like life insurance, if no one is dependent on you, it is only you that needs to worry about it. But if people are dependent on you, you will want what is best for them.

DISABILITY INSURANCE

STUDENT: Disability insurance, yet another pleasant topic to think about.

PROFESSOR: I agree, however it is the one insurance area where most people are significantly underinsured.

S: You know with all these insurances we have covered, auto, home, now disability, and life to follow, I am not going to have any money left to have fun. I certainly won't have money for that policy that covers umbrellas.

P: You'll have plenty of money to have fun as long as you budget and spend it wisely. Remember every financial decision is a trade-off.

S: I'm not planning on being disabled, but what does it all involve?

P: Well no one is planning on being disabled, but current statistics estimate that one in four of today's 20 year olds will become disabled before they retire and the average length of disability is 34.6 months. ("Chances of Disability," n.d.) So, sad to say, you have a 25 percent chance of being disabled before retirement and accidents are not usually the cause. Back injuries, cancer, heart disease are all causes that are more numerous than accidents.

S: You are just full of good news.

P: Don't shoot the messenger. All I can do is make you aware of risks to help ensure that people dependent on you don't suffer significant negative consequences if you have a debilitating injury or disease. Again, if no one is dependent on your income, it is only you that will have a decline in quality of life because of a disability.

S: There must be premiums involved.

P: Absolutely.

S: And deductibles, co-pays, and/or co-insurance.

P: None of those although there is a feature that somewhat serves as a deductible.

S: So how do I get disability insurance?

P: Most people will have it provided by their employers. Approximately 41 percent of employers offer disability insurance. (Andrews, 2017) If your employer does not offer it and you are a professional (lawyer, accountant, and many other professions) chances are your professional association can offer you a policy. You can also buy it as an individual.

Remember the significant difference we saw with respect to medical insurance coverage between large and small employers. I don't have the numbers, but I am confident the same type of differences exists with respect to disability insurance.

S: You said there was no deductible but a feature that serves as a deductible. What would that be?

P: That is the waiting or elimination period. It is the period of time before the disability income starts. It varies by plan and most employers have a short-term disability plan and a long-term disability plan. The short-term plan may generally cover from three months to two years, at which point the long-term plan may kick in.

S: Who determines if I am disabled?

P: A physician can make that determination after an examination and review of all the facts and circumstances. The insurer can always have you reviewed by a physician of their choice after the initial determination and, while you are on disability, have you periodically reviewed by a physician of their choice.

S: I like to ski. If I am severely injured in a skiing accident and will be laid up for six months, can I collect on my disability insurance?

P: Yes you can, but there are circumstances where you cannot collect. For instance, if you are injured while committing a crime, you cannot collect disability income.

S: I don't foresee myself doing that.

P: Glad to hear it.

S: How much does disability income pay?

P: Most policies cover about 60 percent of your gross income, however it differs by policy.

S: Sixty percent, that's it?

P: That's it and if you are a high earner there is a maximum benefit. For instance, if you are making $200,000 per year...

S: I'm hoping to do better down the line.

P: Great, but in the disability income world, whereas the calculation would say you will receive $10,000 per month (($200,000*60%)/12), the policy maximum may be $8,000 per month.

S: That's not fair.

P: Everything factors into the cost of insurance. It is a balancing act between competing interests.

S: Is it taxable?

P: Generally yes, but you know the answer to that.

S: I know...tax course. What about the new tax bill?

P: It addresses part of the equation.

S: Refresh my memory on the equation.

P: Remember it comes down to taxable income, allowable deductions, and credits with all sorts of quirky rules within the categories. I'll always recommend taking the course.

Now back to disability insurance, your employer may have a waiting period of 14 days before the policy kicks in and they will most likely charge you for vacation days while paying you in the interim.

S: What?? They are not taking my vacation days.

P: Well you are not working and are getting paid, so you can have that discussion with them.

Now, as we have discussed, the short-term disability covers a pre-defined period before the long-term kicks in.

S: How long will the long-term last?

P: With many policies it can run until your retirement date.

S: I hope I don't have to use it until then.

P: I certainly hope not, but the protection helps whomever is dependent on you. Certainly their lifestyle will change significantly since you now have significant medical costs, probably up to your "stop loss" each year.

S: Not a pleasant thought.

P: Absolutely not, but a better alternative than not having disability insurance.

S: What other factors determine the cost? I have to guess that the longer the elimination or waiting period, the cheaper the cost since it is effectively a higher deductible.

P: Your progress is great. Your occupation also comes into play. If you are a telephone line person you are at greater risk of injury than a college professor so, everything else being equal, your cost will be higher.

There is also the definition of disability. It may be own occupation or any occupation.

S: What does this entail?

P: Well, let's use the telephone line person as an example. Say a disability prevents him/her from climbing poles, et cetera, but this individual could work in the office fielding service calls, dispatching line people, et cetera. If it is an own occupation policy the person is disabled and can collect under the policy. If the policy is any occupation, the person most likely cannot collect because they can perform other services which are in sync with their skills. Obviously it will come down to judgmental decisions in this area.

S: So logically thinking, an own occupation policy would be more expensive because there is a higher probability of collecting under that policy.

P: Nicely done!

S: The benefit period has to come into play. The longer that benefits can be paid, the more expensive the policy as well as the percentage of income that will be reimbursed. The higher the percentage of income to be paid, the higher the cost.

Now if you are purchasing an individual policy, the higher your income obviously the higher your cost and I have to believe health is a factor in most policies.

P: You are right on both counts.

S: I have to assume once you leave your employer, you no longer have disability insurance. Do you have disability insurance outside of work?

P: You are correct about losing the disability insurance coverage after the end of the month in which you leave. I am guilty of not having disability insurance outside of work which is the problem that most employed people have.

S: I am glad I caught you on something.

P: Always trade-offs, as you have learned.

S: Anything else with respect to disability insurance?

P: As with most of our topics, yes. You can get a residual disability rider within disability insurance. Say you are injured and you need to miss work approximately 25 percent of the time for appointments, doctor's orders, et cetera. You can qualify to have this lost income compensated through this rider.

Lastly, see if your disability insurance has a cost of living adjustment as some policies do and some policies don't.

S: And if it does, it will cost more for sure.

P: You know the relationships well.

S: What's next?

P: How about life insurance?

S: Not sure I am going to like this topic.

LIFE INSURANCE

STUDENT: Why do we need to discuss life insurance? I'm 22 years old and in good health, and quite frankly don't like the thought of discussing my own demise.

PROFESSOR: I certainly can't blame you for that. And, with all due respect, if no one is financially dependent on you and you never see anyone being financially dependent on you, you have absolutely no need for life insurance.

I am going to assume however, that at some future point, someone will be financially dependent on you.

S: Yes, I guess I can see that happening down the line whether it is just my significant other, I get married, children enter the picture, or I have a need to support some relative of mine.

P: That happens to most people at some point. Even if you don't have kids, there may be somebody dependent on you that you don't want to see fall on hard times in the event of losing you.

S: But I have heard from recent graduates that you get your life insurance through work.

P: That is generally the case. The caveat here is that life insurance through work is generally term insurance, meaning once you stop working for them, you no longer have life insurance. Let me come back to that as I want to go through the basic types of life insurance with you.

S: Life insurance is life insurance. Are we talking multiple options and alternatives now?

P: Multiple options and options within options. Remember that you are not going for your PhD in insurance, but are looking to know enough to ask the right questions.

S: I'm actually looking forward to a multiple choice test where there is only one right answer.

P: I'll defer comment on that. The basic types are term and permanent. Within permanent, there are whole life and universal policies so we'll discuss each of these.

S: Okay, let's discuss term first since you already mentioned that it is generally the type of policy that you have with your employer.

P: Glad to see you were listening. Term life means you are covered for a specific period of time. Generally, in the case of being covered under term because of your employment, once you leave this company, you are no longer covered. That said, some group companies will give you the option of converting to permanent life insurance upon leaving the company, but that can be a more expensive alternative.

S: So, using an extreme example, as you so often like to do. If I have $1,000,000 of insurance and my last day of employment is a Friday and I drop dead on Saturday, whoever was to get the money, gets nothing.

P: Sorry for your demise. Your insurance goes to the end of the month in which you leave employment so make sure the above scenario does not occur if Friday is the last day of the month as it will cost your beneficiary $1,000,000. You should have gone before midnight.

S: Thanks for your sympathy! What is a beneficiary?

P: Investment accounts, life insurance accounts, and other financial accounts will always ask you to name a primary beneficiary in the event of your demise.

S: Can I only have one?

P: You can have as many as you want. You can have 100 people getting 1 percent each, 200 people getting 0.5 percent each, et cetera.

S: You are using your extreme examples again.

P: Of course, most insured will have one however, if you are neither married nor have children, you may have all sorts of friends and relatives you want to remember you fondly.

S: I have heard of something called a contingent beneficiary. What is that?

P: The contingent beneficiary receives the proceeds if the primary beneficiary has pre-deceased the insured.

S: Can you change beneficiaries?

P: You absolutely can at any time. I would caution you though not to change beneficiaries on a whim; I would think about it for at least 72 hours and discuss it with a trusted friend or advisor who has no interest in the outcome.

S: What if you don't have a beneficiary named?

P: In that case, the distribution will be determined by the Probate Court of the State. There are different laws for different states. Don't put yourself in that position. You'd rather make the decision than leave it to the courts, which may lead to an outcome you would not have wanted.

S: What if I want to take it with me?

P: There's a good joke which includes a lawyer, accountant, and a priest, but I'll defer to another time on that.

S: Okay, I am ready to be confused. Let's go through the different types of term insurance.

P: You are well beyond where you think you are. I don't think you'll have any problems with this. Term insurance has no investment component. It covers you for a specified period of time as long as you are paying the premiums. All insurance premium payments for all types of policies generally have a 30-day grace period.

S: Meaning?

P: The policy remains in force as long as your latest premium due is not more than 30 days late which cancels the policy.

S: That's lousy.

P: Pay your premiums on time. Think back to the importance of budgeting your money. The two basic types of term are annual renewable term and level premium term.

S: What is annual renewable term?

P: It is term insurance from one year to the next. The problem however is that each year, from an actuarial standpoint, you are one year closer to your ultimate demise so it will cost you a little bit more each year as you age. That said, over any of the periods covered with level premium term to be discussed next, the total cost of annual renewable and level premium won't be much different.

S: I'm lost here.

P: I can see that. Premiums in the early years of annual renewable term will be lower than level premium term, and in later years they will be higher. Big picture, the difference in total over the length of the level term won't be that great.

S: Okay, I understand that, but you mentioned something about an artery standpoint or something I didn't follow. What was that all about?

P: Actuarial standpoint. Actuaries are gifted mathematically and determine probabilities of occurrence for insurance purposes, life expectancies, et cetera. It is a well-paid profession.

S: I'm not ready for that yet. I may possibly take accounting but don't want any math beyond that. What about level premium term?

P: You can buy level premium term for multiyear periods such as five years, 10 years, or 20 years. This is what is recommended for couples with young children as it is much cheaper than whole life and universal life. You make the decision that you want to have coverage before your children are able to be on their own, and you can have much more coverage with these term policies for the same dollars than you would with whole life or universal life.

S: And the cost is the same each year right? If I am following correctly interpreting the term, pun intended, *level* premium.

P: You are correct. Just be aware that the annual cost of a 20 year term will be higher than a 10 year term, which will be higher than a five year term because you are covering a longer period of time. All in all though, the policies are attractively priced.

S: Let's discuss whole life now.

P: With whole life, there is an insurance component and an investment component. Whole life will have a cash value with it and a death value. Term insurance has no cash value. Whole life premiums are generally level from year to year and the cash value is increasing. It also gives you the ability to stop paying yearly premiums and switch to another lower value of coverage. Premiums are payable through age 100, at which point the policy is fully paid.

S: Let's hope I make it to 100.

P: Gives you a much better chance of shooting below your age on the golf course.

S: What do you mean by cash value?

P: Let's look at an actual policy. Here is a policy with a $25,000 death benefit. The premiums, as I said, are payable until the covered

AMICA LIFE INSURANCE COMPANY
ANNUAL BENEFIT STATEMENT

INSURED: POLICY NO.:

MARY A. MC GUINNESS   DATE OF BIRTH:

POLICY ANNIVERSARY: 10/28/2017

PLAN OF INSURANCE: WHOLE LIFE II - (FLEXIBLE PREMIUM WHOLE LIFE POLICY)

COVERAGES	MAXIMUM* AMOUNT OF COVERAGE	ISSUE DATE	PREMIUMS PAYABLE TO	MATURITY/EXPIRY DATE
BASE PLAN	$25,000	10/28/1991		

*PLEASE REVIEW YOUR POLICY FOR COMPLETE DETAILS OF YOUR COVERAGE AMOUNT

BENEFICIARIES:

 RIMARY:
CONTINGENT:

****IMPORTANT BENEFICIARY NOTICE****

PLEASE BE ADVISED THAT MANY STATES' LAWS RESTRICT THE RIGHTS OF AN EX-SPOUSE (AND, IN SOME CASES, HIS OR HER FAMILY MEMBERS) IF SUCH PERSON WAS NAMED AS BENEFICIARY PRIOR TO DIVORCE OR ANNULMENT FROM THE INSURED. PLEASE CONTACT OUR LIFE CUSTOMER SERVICE DEPARTMENT IF YOU HAVE ANY QUESTIONS OR CONCERNS REGARDING THIS MATTER.

POLICYOWNER:
MARY A. MC GUINNESS

SEND PREMIUM NOTICES TO:
MARY A. MC GUINNESS

PREMIUM	PAYMENT FREQUENCY	PAID TO
$175.75	ANNUAL	10/28/2018

POLICY VALUES:

YOUR POLICY IS A PERMANENT PLAN OF INSURANCE WHICH PROVIDES YOU WITH THE FOLLOWING OPTION(S):

- YOU MAY SURRENDER YOUR POLICY AND RECEIVE A CASH VALUE PAYMENT OF $5,416.25, OR

- YOU MAY DISCONTINUE MAKING PREMIUM PAYMENTS AND HAVE A REDUCED FULLY PAID UP PERMANENT LIFE INSURANCE POLICY WITH A DEATH BENEFIT OF $18,766, OR

- YOU MAY DISCONTINUE MAKING PREMIUM PAYMENTS AND HAVE A DEATH BENEFIT OF $25,000 IN FORCE AS EXTENDED TERM INSURANCE FOR 17 YEARS AND 84 DAYS., OR

- YOU MAY CONTINUE MAKING PREMIUM PAYMENTS

ACTUAL VALUES MAY DIFFER, DEPENDING ON THE DATE THE CHANGE IS MADE.

IF YOU SHOULD HAVE ANY QUESTIONS, PLEASE CONTACT OUR LIFE CUSTOMER SERVICE DEPARTMENT AND SPEAK WITH ONE OF OUR SERVICE REPRESENTATIVES AT 800-234-5433, EXTENSION 89075.

individual is 100 years old. As you can see, the primary beneficiaries and contingent beneficiaries are noted. If you go to the next page, you will see that the premium is $175.75 per year.

Following the bullet points, this policy could have been surrendered right at October 28, 2017 for a cash value of $5,416.25.

S: What do you mean by "surrendered?"

P: The person turns in the policy, meaning his/her heirs will not get $25,000 at his/her death. In exchange, the person receives $5,416.25.

The next bullet point gives the person the option of not making any additional premium payments and then his/her heirs will get $18,766 upon his/her death.

The third bullet point means the person can stop making payments and his/her heirs will collect $25,000 if they die within 17 years and 84 days.

S: This is all creepy discussing dying within certain dates to collect, et cetera. Let me understand the third bullet point; the person dies 17 years and 83 days from the anniversary date on this notice and has three heirs. Each heir collects $8,333, but if the person dies 17 years and 85 days from the anniversary date on this notice, each heir gets nothing.

P: You are partially correct. With respect to the 17 years and days comments you are correct. With the distribution, it is what the policy owner has determined. If there are two primary beneficiaries, one getting 75 percent and one getting 25 percent and one contingent beneficiary, the scenario is as follows: To make it easier,

I'll say the primary beneficiary getting 75 percent is A, the primary beneficiary getting 25 percent is B, and C is the contingent beneficiary. We agree that nothing is distributed if death occurs at the 17 years and 85 days previously discussed.

Now, if the death occurs within 17 years and 84 days and A, B, and C are alive, then A gets $18,750, B gets $6,250, and C gets nothing. If either A or B is alive and the other is not, then the one alive will get $25,000. If A and B are both dead at the time of death of the insured, then C gets $25,000.

S: So C is rooting for A and B to die.

P: I would not be so crass. Everyone may not even know they are a primary or contingent beneficiary; it is the policy holder's discretion as to whom they tell what.

S: What if A, B, and C pre-decease the policy holder? Probate?

P: Excellent question and excellent answer. Hopefully, however with this occurrence prior to the death of the last of A, B, and C, the policy holder has named other beneficiaries to avoid probate.

S: Wow, I am not sure I like all these alternatives with respect to death.

P: It is consistent with the multiple alternatives we have seen in every other topic discussed. Think back to the outcome we talked about long ago when we started these discussions. The goal is to put you in a position to ask good questions and do what is best for you and anyone dependent on you.

S: Okay, I understand whole life. Can we talk universal life?

P: Sure, and I will show you what was my actual policy here.

S: What do you mean was your actual policy? It looks like you are still alive and breathing to me.

P: Glad to hear that but, if I had a financial "do over" other than some of my losing stocks, it would be my life insurance selection.

S: You've lost money on some stocks?

P: We discussed this in investing. If you can find me an active investor who has never lost money on an individual stock, I want to meet him or her. Now my financial "do over" involves the selection of universal life. Not all universal is bad, but it was not the right choice for me.

S: You said universal had an investment component.

P: Once again, I am glad to see you were listening.

S: Why did you select universal life and why would you have changed your decision?

P: I selected universal because of the flexibility of the premiums. I wanted the coverage for my wife and kids beyond what I had at work. With universal, once you make the first year premium payment, you have flexibility as long as there is some cash value in the policy.

S: What do you mean by the flexibility in the premiums?

P: Look at page three of the policy where the annual premium is $552. I got this years ago when $552 might not be possible some

POLICY STATUS REPORT   POLICY NO.:

SUMMARY OF POLICY INFORMATION AS OF 09/04/2016:

1. POLICY COVERAGE AS OF THE ABOVE DATE: AMOUNT

    UNIVERSAL LIFE - OPTION A   DEATH BENEFIT $100,000

2. POLICY VALUES AS OF THE ABOVE DATE:

    ACCUMULATION VALUE $8,320.96
    SURRENDER CHARGE   ($0.00)
    INDEBTEDNESS   ($0.00)
    CASH VALUE $8,320.96

3. THE MONTHLY COST OF BASIC INSURANCE AS OF THE ABOVE DATE WAS $0.737 PER $1,000.

4. THE RATE OF INTEREST AS OF THE ABOVE DATE IS 4.50%.

POLICY STATUS REPORT

SUMMARY OF ACTIVITY:

1. FROM 09/05/2015 THROUGH 09/04/2016, THE SUMMARY OF ACTIVITY IS:

DESCRIPTION

PREMIUMS PAID:	$1,000.00
COST OF BASIC INSURANCE:	$814.13
SUPPLEMENTAL BENEFIT CHARGES:	$0.00
PARTIAL SURRENDERS:	$0.00
SURRENDER CHARGES:	$0.00
INTEREST CREDITED:	$332.54

2. FROM 09/05/2015 THROUGH 09/04/2016, THE MONTHLY ACTIVITY WAS:

MONTH	PREMIUMS PAID	COST OF BASIC INSURANCE	SUPPLEMENTAL BENEFIT CHARGES	PARTIAL SURRENDERS	SURRENDER CHARGES	INTEREST CREDITED	%
9/2015	$0.00	$67.68	$0.00	$0.00	$0.00	$28.03	(4.50)
10/2015	$0.00	$67.71	$0.00	$0.00	$0.00	$28.82	(4.50)
11/2015	$0.00	$67.74	$0.00	$0.00	$0.00	$27.75	(4.50)
12/2015	$0.00	$67.77	$0.00	$0.00	$0.00	$28.52	(4.50)
1/2016	$0.00	$67.80	$0.00	$0.00	$0.00	$28.30	(4.50)
2/2016	$0.00	$67.83	$0.00	$0.00	$0.00	$26.34	(4.50)
3/2016	$0.00	$67.86	$0.00	$0.00	$0.00	$28.00	(4.50)
4/2016	$0.00	$67.89	$0.00	$0.00	$0.00	$26.95	(4.50)
5/2016	$0.00	$67.92	$0.00	$0.00	$0.00	$27.70	(4.50)
6/2016	$0.00	$67.94	$0.00	$0.00	$0.00	$26.66	(4.50)
7/2016	$0.00	$67.98	$0.00	$0.00	$0.00	$27.39	(4.50)
8/2016	$1,000.00	$68.01	$0.00	$0.00	$0.00	$28.08	(4.50)

(NUMBERS IN PARENTHESES INDICATE THE EFFECTIVE ANNUAL RATE PAID EACH MONTH.)

3. POLICY LOAN INFORMATION

AS OF 09/05/2015, INDEBTEDNESS WAS $0.00*

LOAN ACTIVITY FOR THE PERIOD WAS:

AMOUNTS BORROWED	$0.00
LOAN REPAYMENTS	$0.00
LOAN INTEREST CHARGED	$0.00

AS OF 09/04/2016 INDEBTEDNESS IS: $0.00

* INCLUDES CAPITALIZED LOAN INTEREST FROM PREVIOUS PERIOD IF UNPAID.

POLICY STATUS REPORT

CURRENT BENEFICIARY:
   PRIMARY:
   CONTINGENT:

CURRENT OWNER:

   MICHAEL J MC GUINNESS

SEND PREMIUM NOTICES TO:

MICHAEL J MC GUINNESS

CURRENT PREMIUMS:

ANNUAL TARGET	$552.00
ANNUAL BILLED PREMIUM	$552.00
PAYMENT FREQUENCY	ANNUAL

***** IMPORTANT NOTICE *****

- MAXIMUM PREMIUM LIMIT FOR THE POLICY YEAR BEGINNING 09/05/2016 IS $13,717.73.

- IF NO FURTHER PREMIUMS ARE PAID, THIS POLICY WILL TERMINATE BY 12/05/2022, PLUS THE GRACE PERIOD, ON A GUARANTEED BASIS

- IF NO FURTHER PREMIUMS ARE PAID, THIS POLICY WILL TERMINATE BY 01/05/2025, PLUS THE GRACE PERIOD, ON A CURRENT BASIS. THIS PROJECTION IS BASED ON CURRENT INTEREST RATES WHICH MAY CHANGE AT ANY TIME.

---

years so I could skip any years where that was the case. Well, what happens with universal is the policy is priced on assumed investment returns. At the time the policy was written, interest rates were quite high so the projected returns on the policy were quite high. As returns drop, the increase in cash value each year would not be as great.

S: If I follow you and this policy correctly, I see on page one that you had $100,000 of coverage. If I, at the same age, wanted a similar policy, it would cost me more than $552 because projected returns have decreased.

P: Great job! You can see that I have a guaranteed rate of 4.5 percent which is well above what you can get from savings now. Your guaranteed rate would be well below that.

S: Why cancel the policy if you have a guaranteed rate of 4.5 percent?

P: Look at the second policy page which shows the insurance cost per month and the interest return. Even though the interest is attractive, you see the insurance cost creeping up each month.

S: I see it but with all due respect Prof, $67.68 from September 2015 to $68.01 in August 2016 is what you would call "chump change."

P: I agree, but can you tell me what my cost in September 2016 would be if you look at the policy?

S: I see on page one it talks about the monthly cost being $0.737 per $1,000 meaning it would be $73.70 in September 2016, which is an increase of $5+ per month.

P: Nicely done.

S: But you can handle a $5 per month increase.

P: Absolutely, but I am hoping to get to an age where I can shoot under my age and that cost will be increasing each year, which means I will need to significantly increase future premium payments. I read too many horror stories about people having to deal with significant increased costs to maintain their universal coverage so I have gone in a different direction.

S: Meaning?

P: I have taken the cash value, invested it at guaranteed rates, and increase it each year by what I would have paid into my policy. In the end, my heirs won't get $100,000, but they should get something as long as I don't need to dig into it.

S: Can we go through the rest of the policy so I understand it?

P: I think you are at the point where you can explain it to me.

S: Okay, looking at page one, you had a $100,000 death benefit and your cash value is $8,320.96. Your new monthly cost would have been $73.70 and your guaranteed interest rate is 4.5 percent.

P: Nice job, keep going.

S: On page two, you paid $1,000 in premiums in the last year, you earned $332.54, and your insurance cost for the year was $814.13. If I follow the logic correctly, your cash value increased by $518.40. I still don't understand why you cancelled the policy if your cash value is increasing and your annual cost is going up by only about $70 in the next year.

P: You are asking the right questions and it was not an easy decision, but at $70 per year for 25 years, how much is the annual increase?

S: I see $1,750 and I am guessing you are thinking the $70 per year increase will be increasing also.

P: Correct! Only time will tell if I made the right decision, but let's continue on with the policy.

S: Okay, continuing on page two, you have no loans. How would you have a loan?

P: With an insurance policy, you can borrow up to the cash value. Please note that if I did that, my effective rate would be 4.5 percent which would be my lost interest on the money no longer invested.

S: On page three, you have a primary and contingent beneficiary (or beneficiaries) as we saw in the whole life example.

I don't understand the maximum premium limit.

P: The most I could put into the policy in the next year would be $13,717.73. This may have been the move to make since I am guaranteed 4.5 percent, but I have to go with the assumption, correctly or incorrectly, that I can do better in the stock market.

S: And your 4.5 percent return would have been reduced by you continuing to pay the annual premium.

P: Excellent! I was not even going to cover that, you are picking things up quite well in big picture terms.

S: Thanks Prof, continuing on, if you did not pay any additional premiums, the policy will terminate by December 5, 2022 plus the grace period on a guaranteed basis.

P: Yes, remember the 30-day grace period?

S: If there are no further premiums paid, the policy will terminate by January 5, 2025 plus the grace period on a current basis. I don't understand this if they are paying you based on the guaranteed rate.

P: Funny, neither could I and I could never get a good answer from the company. My only guess is that the company has assumed rates higher than the guaranteed rate of 4.5% which makes no sense to me.

S: Glad to hear you say you're not sure you made the right move.

P: It is true with many financial decisions. All you can do is ask as many questions as possible and go with what you think is right.

S: Any other insurance possibilities?

P: Actually, when I was traveling overseas quite a bit, the company had a travel policy on me that would have paid my wife seven times my salary if I died on a business trip.

S: Any risk with that?

P: Only if my wife finally realized that I was worth much more dead than alive.

S: What are the key factors determining the cost of an insurance policy?

P: Similar to auto and home insurance, multi variant analysis is used. You can already tell me one key variable that we have discussed.

S: It has to be your age. The younger you are, everything else being equal, the lower it will cost since you have more years to pay.

P: You got it. Other key variables to consider are gender as women outlive men by an average of five years. There are a lot of good jokes here also but I can't tell you any; otherwise, I run the risk of increasing that difference.

S: Smoking has to be a big one.

P: Absolutely, a smoker will pay far more than a non-smoker.

S: Your health?

P: Another big one. If you are heavy or obese, you will pay far more. If you have high blood pressure, diabetes, et cetera, your policy cost will be higher.

S: Isn't that discrimination?

P: It is just what the statistics say and the cost of insurance is based on a multitude of statistics.

S: What else?

P: Your occupation. Certainly a college professor is at much lower risk than someone working as a firefighter, on the police force, or in the military.

Your lifestyle. Are you a major mountain climber, a sky diver, et cetera? Your family medical history will come into play as well as your driving record and a host of other factors.

S: Driving record…Based on everything we have discussed, I can see including it. If you have multiple speeding tickets and/or a couple of DWIs, you are much more at risk.

P: You are seeing the big picture.

S: What else can you tell me about life insurance?

P: Only that I have covered the very basics with you. There are other types of term, whole life, and other life insurance policies such as variable life. I have full confidence that when the time comes, you will ask the right questions, understand the other variations, and make the right decision for you and your heirs.

S: Not sure I am comfortable with planning for my own demise.

P: You shouldn't be, but it is a necessary task and you'll need to make the call as to who you want involved in the discussion.

S: How do I determine how much life insurance I need?

P: Many factors there, most importantly who is dependent on you and their ages. There are many models for how much insurance you should have. Remember back to budgeting; you have many things you need to budget for and life insurance will be one of them. You will find the proper balance. Even at work, you will have the option to buy coverage beyond what is being provided for you by your employer.

Let's look at an employee benefits package now.

REVIEW OF AN EMPLOYEE BENEFITS PACKAGE

PROFESSOR: I am going to review the employee benefits package offered to Saint Anselm employees, which is a good package. You want to review the benefit package before you accept the job offer so you know what your potential out-of-pocket costs are and the risks you have.

STUDENT: I'll just ask for that at the first interview.

P: Never initiate the salary or benefit discussion. They may discuss salary with you; you may need to ask for the benefit package after the job has been offered to you.

S: Well, based on what we have discussed to date, I have an idea of what some of the items may be in a benefit package.

P: You will also see others in this package that I have not explained and please ask questions, like you have consistently been doing, if you need an additional explanation on anything.

S: Will do. I see medical with Harvard Pilgrim Health Care is first. I see I am able to join the medical plan on the first day of the month following 14 days of full time employment. Does this mean if I start in the second half of the month, say January 22, I am not eligible to join the plan until March 1?

P: You've come a long way. I am guessing you can explain most of this to me.

S: They use co-pays which are dependent on who you are seeing. What is a PCP?

P: Primary care physician.

S: I should have known that.

P: No, that was the right question.

S: Why are there three different co-pays for prescriptions and mail-order prescriptions?

P: These are dependent on the type of drug being ordered.

S: Ouch! A $3,000 deductible for an individual and $9,000 for a family? I thought you said this was a good plan.

P: With the cost of health care these days, that would not be great, but still not bad, compared to other options. However, where the excellence of this plan comes into play is in the next bullet point.

S: We did not discuss a health reimbursement arrangement. What is that?

P: Basically, after you have $500 of deductible expenses, Saint Anselm will reimburse you for the next $2,500 per dependent until you hit the $3,000 deductible of the plan.

S: So if I understand this correctly, because of Saint Anselm's generosity, you effectively have a $500 deductible per person?

P: Yes, that is correct.

S: That is a great perk. So if I am on this plan, it will cost me $2,337.96 per year ($194.83 * 12). If it is my spouse and me, I am assuming I cannot put a significant other on the plan, it is $4,675.80 ($389.65 * 12), and if I have a family it is $6,312.36 ($526.03 * 12) per year?

P: You are correct on all counts including that you cannot put a significant other on the plan.

S: What about the number of kids? Any difference between one kid and seven kids?

P: None at all. If you have a lot of kids, you are benefiting from the law of averages; if you have one kid, you are not benefiting by the law of averages. However, one kid or seven kids, it is a very good plan.

S: Dental! I like that. Same reasoning if I start on January 4, I am not eligible until March 1?

P: Very good again.

S: This looks good too, two cleanings per year. I notice there is no co-pay here but there is a deductible depending on type of procedure. Braces are 50 percent covered for the kids up to a $2,000 limit is a nice perk too.

What is the calendar maximum?

P: That is the most that can be spent on any covered person during the year.

S: That's pretty good. And with only a $50 deductible per individual and $150 per family. I can see the costs are reasonable also. Being single it would only cost me $164.64 a year and it looks reasonable for a family also.

P: You are developing a good instinct for benefit plans.

S: Vision too? Eligibility period consistent with dental I see.

P: Pun intended?

S: I've been listening to you for too long and tired of being punished.

P: Not bad.

S: Only a $10 co-pay for an eye exam. That's great! The $130 allowance is towards frames after which it looks like you get a 20 percent discount off the balance.

P: You are very good at reading this benefit summary.

S: I am understanding it and I see it is even more generous for contact lenses as you can get new ones every 12 months instead of every 24. Only $73.56 per year for me, sign me up.

P: I agree, it is a good plan for vision. What's next?

S: Oh no! Life insurance, back to planning for my demise.

P: Well, it is free, so even if no one is dependent on you, hopefully you can find a beneficiary or two to name.

S: Sounds quite morbid. No one wants to profit from my death.

P: No they don't, but always take advantage of any benefit offered for free if you can. Name your favorite charity as your beneficiary if you want.

S: That's not a bad idea.

P: I'll take that as a little bit of praise.

S: So they will cover me up to one and a half times my salary. If I am making $50,000 and meet my maker, my beneficiary (or beneficiaries) will get $75,000. I see it is limited to a $200,000 maximum like you mentioned when we spoke about life insurance.

P: You are correct about the $75,000 and you are correct about the maximum.

S: You know, we have talked a lot about taxes and I don't remember if we discussed if life insurance is taxed.

P: Life insurance proceeds are always tax free.

S: Whether $75,000 or $1,000,000?

P: That is correct.

S: What is AD&D?

P: Before we get into that, I want to point out that you can buy additional life insurance in the amount of one, one and a half, or two times salary. It is just additional term insurance.

S: So someone can make even more from my demise.

P: It is a good option if someone is dependent on you, although since you are buying additional term, you may want to look at other policies that will carry forward with you if you change jobs. This option would not.

S: Got it. What about the AD&D?

P: It is accidental death and dismemberment.

S: I am not sure I am going to like this topic. What do you mean by dismemberment?

P: Well, you are covered for accidental death and also if you lose any bodily function, such as the ability to see, or a body part such as an arm or a leg.

S: I get paid if I lose an arm?

P: That is correct.

S: How much?

P: It is dependent on the policy. The policy will have a monetary value for each of the body parts that you could lose.

S: This is pretty sick.

P: It is the insurance world and certainly if you lose a body part, some financial compensation will help.

S: Short-term disability! We covered that. Wow, it doesn't kick in until the first of the month following one year of full time employment, and that is the same for long term. I remember you telling me that this is where most Americans are underinsured and now I can see why.

P: Glad you have remembered prior discussions again, and this provision is pretty standard. Remember there is risk to an employer when hiring a new employee, and this provision serves to mitigate that risk.

S: Okay, 60 percent is the standard as we discussed and there is a $7,000 maximum per month, and the short-term covers six months after a 15-day waiting period. I remember that is the disability equivalent of a deductible.

P: Correct, and hopefully the employee has enough vacation and sick days to carry them through that 15-day period so there is no loss of income.

S: Let me see if I really understand this area. With a $7,000 maximum and 60 percent covered, you will get the 60 percent up to a salary of $140,000 per year. (($7,000/.6)*12) If you are making more than $140,000, you are limited to the $7,000 per month.

P: You have the foundation I was hoping you would develop. Nicely done!

S: Long term, it will cover you up to age 65. Not a pleasant thought!

P: You certainly hope it does not come to that.

S: What about after age 65?

P: You should be picked up on Medicare for health and probably Social Security Disability Income. You will suffer a significant drop-off though in your monthly cash flow.

S: Flexible spending accounts for health and dependent care with eligibility on the first day of the month after 30 days of full-time employment. I don't remember us talking about a flexible spending account.

P: We haven't. Basically you can have up to $2,650 deducted spread over your paychecks for the year which will go to covering your non-reimbursed out-of-pocket expenses for medical, dental, and vision expenses, as well as co-pays for prescription drugs.

S: So it is like a savings account to cover my deductibles, co-pays, and co-insurance?

P: You're half-right on this comment. You will get reimbursed for your deductibles, co-pays, co-insurance, and any medical costs not covered by the plan. You can even use it for certain medical supplies such as contact lens solution and band-aids.

S: Understood, but why are you saying I am half-right?

P: Because it is use it or lose it. If you have $2,650 deducted and only have $1,500 of out-of-pocket costs, you do not get $1,150 back.

S: What do you mean I don't get it back?

P: That is why it is called "use it or lose it."

S: This makes no sense whatsoever. Why would I take this risk of having money deducted when I can just pay it as it arises and eliminate this risk?

P: You are asking the right questions which I am glad to see, and what course have I been continually telling you to take?

S: The tax class, but I don't see how it is relevant here.

P: Well the $2,650 is a tax benefit. It reduces your annual taxable income.

S: So if I am making $50,000 and have $2,650 deducted, I am only taxed on $47,350?

P: Correct on the federal and state level; you will still be paying Social Security and Medicare on the $2,650.

S: My head is spinning again. What is the right number to deduct?

P: It is completely dependent on your projected medical expenses for the year and your marginal tax rate.

S: How the heck does marginal tax rate figure into this?

P: Just like with municipal bonds, I'll do one exercise with you assuming a 22% marginal tax bracket. If you have $2,000 deducted, how much do you save in taxes?

S: Duh, $440.

P: No need to be a smart aleck here. So what is your out of pocket spending now for the year?

S: I apologize, no disrespect intended. $2,000 deducted minus $440 less in federal taxes means I am out $1,560.

P: Great so if your reimbursable expenses are less than $1,560, you left some money on the table. If your reimbursable expenses are between $1,560 and $2,000, you benefited from the plan. If your reimbursable expenses are over $2,000, you benefited by $440 but passed up the opportunity to save more.

S: You know the scary part of this is that I just understand what you did.

P: Not scary and what else can you tell me with respect to this?

S: That you will get different answers with different marginal tax rates.

P: Very impressive indeed, and you didn't think you knew anything about taxes.

S: But tax simplification changes all of this.

P: The only thing tax simplification changes with respect to this is the marginal tax rates. The concepts remain.

S: So what is the right answer to deduct?

P: It is different for everyone based on their projected expenses. Personally I think the best thing to do is not to overpay meaning in the above example, your after-tax contribution is greater than your expenses. If you could have saved more, that would have helped but you have not suffered any out of pocket loss.

S: Anything else?

P: The beauty here is you have until March 15 of the following year to incur medical expenses. So if you have some discretionary medical costs, get the work done before March 15.

S: I don't understand this.

P: Say you had $1,500 deducted and as of December 31, you have $1,300 in reimbursable medical expenses. If you have work you need done in the next year, get it done before March 15 as the first $200 will count towards the just completed year and the balance will count towards the next year's flexible spending account.

S: How do I get reimbursed?

P: Just keep a file with your reimbursable expenses, document them, and turn copies into the plan administrator and voila, a check magically appears in the mail on a very timely basis. This is the way a dinosaur like me does it. You would probably elect to have a debit card to access the money in your account.

S: I am glad you have finally admitted you are a dinosaur.

P: Yes, but that only makes it more painful when you take a beating on the golf course.

S: We'll see about that, but I do understand this now. What about the dependent care FSA?

P: Same principle except it can be for elder care or child care and you can have $5,000 deducted pre-tax for it.

S: So if I am in the 22 percent tax bracket and have $5,000 deducted, I am saving $1,100 in taxes and I can be reimbursed up to $5,000 for bills to take care of my parents or kids?

P: Yes, that is correct.

S: Employee assistance program?

P: Trusted personnel you or any member of your covered family can call at any time. If you feel you have a drinking or drug problem, depression, et cetera, every discussion is confidential with trained professionals and they will try to determine, with you, the best resources to help you.

S: 403(b) retirement plan. My eligibility is consistent with other programs within this package. The college starts to contribute after two years with the first of the month proviso. What exactly is a 403(b) retirement plan?

P: It is the non-profit equivalent of a 401k plan.

S: So it is pre-tax if my gross is $50,000 and I elect to contribute 10 percent to the 403(b), then I am taxed at the federal level on $45,000?

P: Very good, so you know what you saved in taxes based on?

S: My marginal tax rate.

Now, I see where Saint A's will match 50 percent of my first 3 percent, meaning 1.5 percent and then Saint A's contributes another 7 percent, meaning if I have 3 percent deducted, Saint A's puts in 8.5 percent and I am saving 11.5 percent of my gross.

P: That is absolutely correct.

S: That is great.

P: It is good. Remember there is no pension plan nor would I expect there to be as a college or university does not want to assume the risks and potential financial burden with a pension plan. Many companies are dropping them. The lack of a pension plan makes you responsible for funding your own retirement.

If you don't put at least the 3 percent in, I am going to see if I can get your future degree revoked when you make that decision. Hopefully you are putting in more.

S: Tuition remission, if you work at Saint A's, your spouse or dependent children get to go to the school for free? What a great benefit.

P: It absolutely is.

S: What is non-exempt staff and why do they need three years of full-time employment versus one year for faculty and exempt administrators?

P: Generally non-exempt staff are paid on an hourly basis and exempt staff are salaried. There may be some other differentiations. With respect to your second question, I don't know. I will say it is most likely consistent with other schools. Do note that the employee is eligible, the different treatment relates to the spouse and children.

S: What is the second tuition remission program?

P: There is a group of approximately 567 colleges that eligible children of Saint A's employees can go to tuition-free, assuming adequate space exists.

S: So there are no guarantees?

P: None, but it is certainly a great benefit when it works.

S: Vacation time. How is this plan?

P: Comparable to plans elsewhere.

S: So if I understand this, a non-exempt employee in their third year would get 12 days of vacation while exempt administrators would get 15 days?

P: That is correct.

S: Again, the difference. Why a difference?

P: Good question. I will tell you that this is not uncommon as, similar to the tuition remission, many companies offer different benefits to salaried employees and hourly employees. You'll want to keep this in mind when reviewing the benefits package offered to you.

S: Sick leave, six days per year and 14.5 holidays per year. Is this good or bad?

P: Very good.

S: Looks like some good additional benefits.

P: There absolutely are, particularly the fitness center. After the first two weeks of each semester, the crowd really starts to thin out.

Before moving on to our next topic, I want you to know about IRAs, Roth IRAs, and Roth 401ks.

S: What is an IRA?

P: An IRA is an individual retirement account. It is used primarily by individuals who do not have access to a 401k or 403b through their employer. Specific maximums of money can be put aside each year dependent on income levels, and the deductions can reduce taxable income.

S: So for AGI!

P: You will do very well in the tax class, but not better than the classics major for sure.

S: I'll see about that.

P: Big picture, while amounts put in an IRA or 401k are deductible in computing taxes, amounts put into a Roth IRA or Roth 401k are not.

S: So why would I ever contribute to a Roth IRA or Roth 401k rather than an IRA or 401k (or 403b for a non-profit)?

P: Because when money is withdrawn from the Roth accounts, it is not taxed. When withdrawn from an IRA, 401k, or 403b, it is taxed. There are rules with respect to income levels for contributions, when you can take withdrawals, et cetera but those are the basics. The tax course will certainly fill you in on the specifics.

S: I feel my head spinning again and I know marginal tax rates come into play but, as you like to say, "big picture," which is better?

P: You correctly note that marginal tax rates come into play. You will know your marginal tax rate when you contribute, but can only project what it might be when you withdraw. That said, most advisors agree that for your age group, the Roth will be the better option.

S: But no certainties, right?

P: You have learned well, and a significant uncertainty is that a future Congress may change the rules with respect to these.

S: I know you have been wanting to discuss student loans and financial aid, but I have to confess: I now realize how lucky I have been in that my parents paid for most of my college costs. I think I know how to ask good questions now and have a cousin, Olivia, who is a junior in high school who won't be as lucky as me. Can we discuss financial aid and student loans so I can help her?

P: Thanks for your candidness, and I am glad you realize how fortunate you are. I know you will ask good questions and give your cousin good guidance so let's discuss those areas now.

Medical – Harvard Pilgrim Health Care — www.harvardpilgrim.org

Eligibility Date	1st day of the month following 14 days of full-time employment
Benefit	• $25 copay for PCP visits, $50 copay for Specialist visits, $50 copay for Urgent Care Clinic visits • $15 / $25 / $40 copay for prescriptions, $30 / $50 / $120 copay for mail-order prescriptions (90 day supply) • $3,000 individual / $9,000 family calendar-year deductible applies to inpatient care, ambulance, emergency room care, radiology, lab services performed at a hospital facility, and outpatient surgery performed at a hospital facility • Health Reimbursement Arrangement (HRA) administered by CGI Business Solutions reimburses covered members for final $2,500 of incurred deductible expenses per calendar year; members are responsible for paying the first $500 of deductible expenses • Low-Cost Providers (LP) offer cost savings on lab services and outpatient surgery
Cost to Employee	Individual: $194.83 per month Two-Person: $389.65 per month Family: $526.03 per month

Dental – Northeast Delta Dental — www.nedelta.com

Eligibility Date	1st day of the month following 30 days of full-time employment
Benefit	• 100% coverage for diagnostic and preventive procedures, including two (2) cleanings in a 12-month period • 80% coverage for basic procedures, including restorative treatment, oral surgery, endodontics, periodontics, denture repair, and emergency palliative treatment • 50% coverage for major restorative procedures after 12-month waiting period • 50% coverage for orthodontics, up to a $2,000 per patient lifetime maximum, for children up to age 19 after a 12-month waiting period • $2,000 calendar year maximum per person; $50 individual / $150 family deductible per calendar year • Health through Oral Wellness (HOW) program
Cost to Employee	Individual: $13.72 per month Two-Person: $25.16 per month Family: $42.21 per month

Vision – DeltaVision — www.eyemedvisioncare.com

Eligibility Date	1st day of the month following 30 days of full-time employment
Benefit	• $10 copay for in-network eye exams • $130 allowance every 24 months towards frames, then 20% balance; $25 copay for standard plastic lenses • $130 allowance every 12 months towards contact lenses in lieu of spectacles, then 15% off balance
Cost to Employee	Individual: $6.13 per month Two-Person: $10.52 per month Family: $18.82 per month

Basic Life and AD&D Insurance – Reliance Standard Life Insurance — www.reliancestandard.com

Eligibility Date	1st day of the month following 30 days of full-time employment
Benefit	Group term life insurance provided in the amount of 1.5 times annual base salary, up to $200,000 maximum
Cost to Employee	None

Voluntary Life and AD&D – Reliance Standard Life Insurance — www.reliancestandard.com

Eligibility Date	1st day of the month following 30 days of full-time employment
Benefit	• Optional supplemental insurance available for purchase in the amount of 1, 1.5, or 2 times annual base salary • Optional spouse life insurance and child life insurance available for purchase • Voluntary amounts are subject to completion of Evidence of Insurability and approval by Reliance Standard
Cost to Employee	Employee paid; cost per schedule

Short-Term Disability – Saint Anselm College

Eligibility Date	1st day of the month following one year of full-time employment
Benefit	Replaces up to 60% of base pay, not to exceed $7,000 per month, for up to 6 months after 15 calendar-day elimination period
Cost to Employee	None

Long-Term Disability – Reliance Standard
www.reliancestandard.com

Eligibility Date	1st day of the month following one year of full-time employment
Benefit	Replaces up to 60% of base pay, not to exceed $7,000 per month, up to age 65 after 6 months of disability
Cost to Employee	None

Flexible Spending Accounts (FSA) – CGI Business Solutions
www.cgibusinesssolutions.com

Eligibility Date	1st day of the month following 30 days of full-time employment
Benefit	• **Health FSA** (annual maximum of $2,600) for out-of-pocket medical, dental, vision and hearing expenses • **Dependent Care FSA** (annual maximum of $5,000) for elder care or child care expenses
Cost to Employee	Employee paid; cost based on employee's annual election

Employee Assistance Program (EAP) – Anthem EAP
www.anthemeap.com

Eligibility Date	Immediate upon hire
Benefit	Offers free, 24/7 confidential support and consultation services to employees and their household members
Cost to Employee	None

403(b) Retirement Plan – TIAA
www.tiaa.org

Eligibility Date	**Employee Contributions:** 1st day of the month following 30 days of full-time employment and 21 years of age **College Contributions:** 1st day of the month following 2 years of full-time employment and 21 years of age (waiting period waived with 2 years of full-time service at a higher education institution within the previous 5 years; eligible 1st of month following 30 days)
Benefit	• Employees may elect to defer pre-tax dollars or contribute Roth post-tax dollars towards retirement • Saint Anselm College matches a maximum of 50% up to the first 3% of eligible employee contributions • Saint Anselm College also provides a flat 7% contribution to eligible employees

Tuition Remission at Saint Anselm College
www.anselm.edu

Eligibility Date	**Non-Exempt Staff:** employee eligible after one year of full-time employment; spouse and dependent children eligible after three years of full-time employment **Faculty and Exempt Administrators:** employee, spouse and dependent children eligible after one year of full-time employment
Benefit	100% tuition for employee, spouse and dependent children at Saint Anselm College; applies to full-time and part-time study

Tuition Remission and Tuition Exchange Programs – NHCUC, CIC-TEP and TE

Eligibility Date	**NHCUC:** dependent children of non-exempt staff, faculty and administrators eligible after one year of full-time employment; **CIC-TEP:** spouses and dependent children of non-exempt staff, faculty and administrators eligible after one year of full-time employment; **TE:** dependent children of faculty and administrators eligible after one year of full-time employment (non-exempt staff not eligible)
Benefit	100% tuition remission for dependents at participating institutions; benefit is subject to approval by host institution

Time Off Benefits

Eligibility Date	1st full calendar month of full-time employment
Benefit	• **Vacation Time:** Non-Exempt Staff • Year 1 through Year 4: accrue 1 day per month, up to 12 days • Year 5 through Year 15: accrue 1.25 days per month, up to 15 days • Year 16+: accrue 1.66 days per month, up to 20 days • **Vacation Time:** Exempt Administrators • Year 1 through 1st Year: accrue 1 day per month, up to 12 days • Year 2 through Year 5: accrue 1.25 days per month, up to 15 days • Year 6+: accrue 1.66 days per month, up to 20 days • **Sick Leave:** accrue ½ day per calendar month, up to a maximum of 40 days • **Holidays:** up to 14.5 holidays per calendar year

Additional Benefits

Dining Hall discounts, Library privileges, Bookstore and Dana Center discounts, Fitness Center privileges, local discounts, and more!

This is a brief outline of benefits and is not intended to contain complete information. Contact the Office of Human Resources for the staff handbook and/or benefit plan documents for more detailed information. Saint Anselm College reserves the right to make changes to its benefits plans at any time. Rev 10/2017

PAYING FOR SCHOOL AND FINANCIAL AID

STUDENT: Well I am thinking back to when we were discussing the power of compound interest and you told me the "all in" cost of Saint A's has increased at an annualized rate of approximately 6.84 percent over a 40 year period.

PROFESSOR: Phenomenal isn't it? And other schools have gone up at a much higher rate and you know what a 1 percent difference means over 40 years.

S: So how does my cousin Olivia handle the price of college?

P: Very carefully. Do you remember what I told you when we were discussing car buying?

S: One thing was never to pay sticker price.

P: Well, in that aspect, college pricing is like car pricing. There is the sticker price and there is the real price. The key for Olivia is to come in with a strong background, grades, extracurricular activities, et cetera and look to receive merit aid and other types of aid that reduce the sticker price. This is called "net price." There is a net price calculator on every college that awards financial aid in the United States.

Also, similar to car buying, as much as she might like a school, if she has a much better deal somewhere else, she needs to carefully consider it.

Make sure she investigates scholarships offered in your local community, especially organizations to which her parents belong. The Knights of Columbus, Elks, Moose...

S: Lions and tigers and bears too?

P: Funny guy! There are lots of fraternal organizations, women's groups, sports groups, et cetera that offer scholarships. Due diligence is necessary here.

S: Where else?

P: She needs to use her search powers, which are far superior to mine. At www.unigo.com/scholarship, I found a scholarship for $2,500 for having the best essay to the question, "Which superhero would you like to change places with for a day and why?" www.fastweb.com is another popular scholarship search engine.

S: Now you're being the funny guy.

P: No, there are all sorts of unique scholarships available. Olivia needs to do her homework and you never know what she might find. After all scholarships, now she needs to look at student loans and grants. I am taking work-study as a given that she will do.

S: Okay, I am ready to discuss student loans.

P: Funny, you probably know more about them than me. What is the one course I have been consistently telling you to take?

S: Taxes, why?

P: Well, I need to go take a course on student loans. After reading what I have read, taxes would be a simple course compared to a course on student loans. That said, let's review the area.

The starting point for federal student loans is the Free Application for Federal Student Aid (FAFSA). The web address is www.fafsa.ed.gov. If Olivia wants financial aid, she and her parents will need to complete this.

S: Is it easy?

P: It is supposed to get easier. I have filled out more than my fair share for my own children and those of others, and I far prefer a tax return.

S: What does the FAFSA do?

P: It will calculate the expected family contribution (EFC), which is a needs analysis tool. It is a family contribution as the calculation considers components of the income and assets of the parents and the student. The FAFSA alone does not create eligibility for federal aid.

S: What else is involved in creating eligibility for federal aid?

P: It is a combination of factors involving the cost of attendance at the college, minus the family contribution minus other resources offered which creates eligibility for the subsidized loan.

S: What is a subsidized loan?

P: A loan in which the federal government is subsidizing part of the interest cost. The government pays the interest until the loan becomes due. I'll discuss this in a little bit.

S: How accurate did you find the expected family contribution?

P: Well, I always liked to joke with other parents, who readily concurred, that we would need to lay off the butler and chauffer in order to reach the EFC but that said…you always find a way.

S: What is the most popular type of loan?

P: By far, it is the Federal Direct Loan (Fay, n.d.) which in 2017 had 32.8 million students borrowing a total of $705.3 billion (U.S. Department of Education, n.d.) , so we will review these first. Just to be accurate, the numbers with respect to 2017 are still not finalized however, give you a good order of magnitude.

The one that is definitely preferable is the Direct Subsidized Loan. I'll focus first on this, which covers dependent students whose parents are able to obtain a Parent Loan for Undergraduate Students (PLUS) loan. We'll discuss the PLUS loan now.

S: Are we talking a lot of acronyms again in discussing financial aid?

P: Unfortunately, yes. So let's say that Olivia and her parents can get a PLUS loan, however she also qualifies for a subsidized loan based on the FAFSA.

S: Sorry to interrupt, but you mentioned you would discuss when a subsidized loan becomes due? Can you discuss that now?

P: Sure, the loan becomes due six months after a student drops below half-time enrollment, withdraws, or graduates. Obviously the goal is after graduation.

S: That is going to be a good chunk of interest paid by the government.

P: I'm glad you appreciate that. Please note that I am only going to discuss undergraduate students. There are different rules for graduate or professional students but, like many other areas we have covered, the concepts remain the same.

Now back to the PLUS loan, in the first year, she can borrow up to $5,500 of which $3,500 may be eligible to be subsidized. That number increases to $6,500 in the second year ($4,500 may be eligible to be subsidized), and $7,500 in years three and four ($5,500 may be eligible to be subsidized each year).

S: What if she wants to be on the five-year plan?

P: Great, if I were her parent I would have no problem with that, as long as she is paying for year five herself. That said, if she has to take a fifth year and takes a loan each year, the maximum loan she may take is an additional $4,000 (aggregate limit of $31,000 of which $23,000 is subsidized).

S: Understood. What is the interest rate on the loan?

P: For the 2017–2018 academic year (July 1, 2017–June 30, 2018), it is 4.45 percent and that loan rate will stay with the amount borrowed each year. It changes each year, but will always be fixed related to that year's borrowing.

S: Does Olivia have to pay off the interest on the unsubsidized balance?

P: No, that can be added to the loan balance, but it would help to pay back what she can. Remember way back when we discussed the benefits of compound interest?

S: I certainly do. Those numbers were eye-opening.

P: I am glad you remember. Now, however, compound interest is working against Olivia, hence the goal to pay as much as she can.

S: Any other costs?

P: There is a loan origination fee of 1.066 percent for loans disbursed October 1, 2017–September 30, 2018 and this also changes every year.

S: How is the origination fee paid?

P: It will be deducted from the disbursement to her school so if she is a junior in college borrowing $7,500, she will be credited by her school as having paid $7,420.05. ($7,500 - ($7,500 * 0.01066))

S: What if her parents don't qualify for a PLUS loan?

P: Then she is able to borrow a bit more. In the first year, she can borrow $9,500 (up to $3,500 subsidized), the second year $10,500 (up to $4,500 subsidized), and $12,500 (up to $5,500 subsidized) in years three and four.

S: What could cause her parent not to qualify for a PLUS loan?

P: Her parents can't get a PLUS loan if they have bad credit unless they have an endorser (effectively a co-signer guaranteeing the loan), or there are extenuating circumstances causing the bad credit.

S: How much can be borrowed under the PLUS loan?

P: This is the scary part to me. The cost of attendance at the school (as determined by the school) minus all other financial aid received can be borrowed by the student.

S: So if the cost of attendance is $50,000 and she has a $5,500 direct loan, then $44,500 can be borrowed for the difference?

P: That is correct, if she does not receive any other forms of financial aid, and for that type of money on the line, Olivia had certainly be spending a lot of time studying in the library.

S: I haven't found that building yet, but I know where the pub is. What is the interest rate on this loan?

P: I know you are kidding, and the interest rate is reset every year, however it remains fixed for the amount borrowed each year. So for a loan from July 1, 2017 through June 30, 2018, the rate will always be 7 percent.

S: And a small loan origination fee?

P: Not quite. The loan origination fee, reset every year, is 4.264 percent for loans disbursed October 1, 2017 through September 30, 2018.

S: So for a $20,000 loan, the origination fee is $852.80. ($20,000 * 0.04264) Ouch!

P: All the more reason for Olivia to get as much as she can in scholarships, grants, work-study, everything under the sun.

S: How does she go about repaying a federal direct loan?

P: That's the right question.

She has different options. She can select the option that is best for her and she can change her option if another alternative becomes more viable.

The standard repayment plan is over 10 years. With a consolidation loan, which we will discuss, it can be up to 30 years. With the 10 year plan, she'll be paying the same amount each year similar to a mortgage. Likewise on the 30 year plan.

S: Thirty years on a mortgage and 30 years on a student loan. I am not sure I am liking this option for Olivia.

P: All the more reason to thank your parents. She'll make the right decision when the time is right. Let me explain other potential repayment plans for the federal direct loan, whether subsidized or unsubsidized since they are the most popular.

There is a graduated repayment plan which is over 10 years. The payments start out lower and then increase generally every two years.

There is an extended repayment plans which is over 25 years. Because of the interest component, like a 30 versus 15 year mortgage, she'll end up paying more.

There is an income-based repayment plan where she will pay 10 percent to 15 percent of discretionary income each year. If Olivia hasn't paid off the loan after 20–25 years, depending on the circumstances, the balance of the loan may be forgiven.

And, last but not least, there is an income contingent repayment plan. With this, her repayment each year is the lesser of 20 percent of her discretionary income, or the amount she would repay each year with a fixed payment over 12 years.

S: These are all the repayment plans just for a federal direct loan?

P: Yes, and some of these are applicable to other loans. Additionally, there are other repayment options for other loans. I won't go through all these as I see your eyes glazing over. When the time is right, she can review and talk with the loan servicer and others to figure out what the best plan for her might be.

S: Thanks for not going over any others, my head is already spinning. But one other question please: Is discretionary income for a student loan repayment the same as discretionary income when we talked about budgeting so long ago?

P: Good question, and the answer is no. I hate to tell you this though, there are two different definitions of discretionary income which are dependent on the loan repayment plan.

S: I thought you were kidding when you said this was harder than taxes. Taxes are about to become much easier now though, right? Even though you have been hinting that might not be true.

P: You never know. Many times, tax simplification leads to more complications. At first glance, I'd say yes, but time will tell.

Now, back to discretionary income. For an income-based repayment plan and a few of the other repayment plans, discretionary income is annual income less 150 percent of the poverty line for Olivia's family size and dependent on the state in which she lives. For an income contingent repayment plan, the definition is the same except that it is less 100 percent rather than 150 percent.

S: What about the forgiveness of loans I heard some of my friends talking about?

P: This would be the Public School Loan Forgiveness Program (PSLF). It forgives the remaining balance if the borrower has made 120 payments under a qualifying repayment plan while working for a qualifying employer.

S: So, if I understand this correctly, she could be on a 30 year repayment plan, but if she works for a qualifying employer, she can have the remaining 20 years of payments wiped out?

P: Not a bad deal. I wish I could have done that with my mortgage, and many of my colleagues and others that have gone before you wished they had that option.

S: Who are the qualifying employers?

P: Federal, state, local, and tribal government organizations.

Most not-for-profits are 501(c) (3) organizations. The following are qualifying employers:

non-taxable groups providing services such as emergency management, military service, public safety, law enforcement, public interest law services, early childhood education, working with individuals with disabilities, or working with the elderly.

The loan forgiveness option is an excellent recruiting tool for these groups so they will be able to tell her if they are a qualified organization.

In addition, the Peace Corps and AmeriCorps are eligible organizations. But for most of these volunteers, they have the option of applying the benefit as a scholarship or loan repayment.

I do want you to understand grants though because they do not have to be repaid. These are contingent on her school being in the program and there is a fixed amount of funds, so once they are gone there is nothing left.

S: Grants sound much better than loans to me.

P: As they should. There are Federal Pell Grants which have a current year maximum of $5,920 for undergraduate studies.

There is the Federal Supplemental Educational Opportunity Grant which provides from $100 to $4,000.

S: I'd prefer the upper end of that range rather than the lower.

P: There are TEACH Grants. TEACH grants can be up to $4,000 per year. Olivia would have to sign an agreement that she will fulfill a specified, to be determined, teaching area for four years within the eight years after graduation. Have Olivia read the fine print carefully here because the grant can revert to a loan and the interest accrued retroactively as of the date of the first disbursement.

There is a grant that a student may be eligible for if her parent or guardian died in military service in Iraq or Afghanistan.

An excellent website where information can be obtained about federal loan repayment plans is www.ifap.ed.gov.

S: What about private loans?

P: She can certainly try to get a private loan for education, but her parents will probably have to co-sign the loan. Olivia would certainly want to exhaust all her federal loan opportunities before she pursues a private loan as it will be more costly, unless her parents have excellent credit. She will not have much flexibility with respect to payments and it will not be forgiven.

Some parents are already borrowing via home equity loans in order to finance college so I hope that is appreciated.

S: I had heard that interest on a home equity loan is tax deductible.

P: It was through the end of 2017, but the new tax bill ended its deductibility except for certain circumstances that do not include college loans.

S: I know, I know what you are going to say, so I will cut you off before you can say it.

P: Good move!

S: After all the borrowing, how much debt does the average college graduate have?

P: The average class of 2016 graduate had $37,172 in student loan debt, up 6 percent from the prior year. ("Look at the Shocking, n.d.)

S: That is scary, I am doubly grateful to my parents now. I thought you did not know anything about financial aid.

P: There are some excellent websites available which I found fairly easily, and I am quite lucky to have very gracious people in the Financial Aid Office at Saint A's who were quite patient with me.

S: So it was like you were in school?

P: Yes it was and, with all due respect to those very gracious people, the tax course is much easier for me than financial aid.

In summary, there are many opportunities out there but Olivia needs to do her…?

S: Due diligence!

P: Glad to see you remember that. Definitely applicable in every area of personal finance.

FINDING A FINANCIAL ADVISOR

PROFESSOR: Well, it has been a long discussion and we are at our final topic, for which you may be grateful. Care to guess what there are a lot of in our final discussion?

STUDENT: Well based on our many topics, I'll have to go with acronyms and questions.

P: Great guesses, but this time I won't be the one with the questions. I'll defer to someone far more knowledgeable than I in this area.

S: What, you don't know the process for finding a financial advisor? Do you have one?

P: I know the process, but I don't have one. Maybe at some point, but since I have not been through the process, I will be a student here also.

S: So what you're telling me is that not everyone needs a financial advisor.

P: Correct, but once you start accumulating significant assets, if you don't have the expertise yourself, it may be a good time to build a relationship with an advisor which hopefully will be a long-term relationship.

S: Word of mouth here, like other topics?

P: I'll give you a yes with extreme caution. Unfortunately, most Ponzi schemes come about because of word of mouth.

S: A what scheme?

P: A Ponzi scheme. Have you heard of Bernie Madoff?

S: Yes, he's the guy who ripped off a lot of people for a lot of money.

P: A fairly concise summary. It was a classic Ponzi scheme and took advantage of a lot of very rich and intelligent people because of the word-of-mouth factor.

S: So how does it work? And I assume you are going to keep it simple like many other topics.

P: Absolutely, we'll call the bad actor Bernie for the sake of argument. Bernie concocts an "investment scheme" and persuades 10 of his friends to invest $10 each for well above average returns. We'll call them Group A. Bernie then finds 10 more people willing to invest $10 each for Group B, and manages to give a dollar back to everyone in Group A. How much money has Bernie received, and how much has he paid out?

S: Well he has taken in $100 from Group A and $100 from Group B so he has taken in $200 and paid out $10.

P: Well done. Now Group A investors have already received a return of 10 percent in short order, so they are happy and now Bernie finds 10 more investors to make up Group C and takes in another $100. He gives another $10 to Group A and $10 to Group B so he has now taken in $300 and paid $30. Meanwhile, Bernie spent $200 for something for himself.

S: And now Group A is raving about a 20 percent short term return and Group B is thrilled with a 10 percent return so Groups D, E, and F want in on the action. When does it end?

P: Only when Bernie runs out of new groups.

S: How did his go so long?

P: Because he was pulling money from both middle income and wealthy people from around the country who were thrilled to become part of his group. He had false statements prepared for customers showing abnormal returns.

The scary part was there was a gentleman in Boston, Harry Markopolos, (Weidner, 2010) who smelled a fraud, and took it upon himself to contact the Securities and Exchange Commission (SEC). They investigated once or twice and found nothing amiss.

S: Moral of the story is you are responsible for doing your own "due diligence."

P: You're making me proud, we discuss it a bit more at the end of this topic. Now on to some acronyms.

First there are registered representatives (RR), formerly known as stockbrokers. If you feel competent buying and selling stocks on your own, you can do so online via Fidelity, Putnam, et cetera so no issues here.

S: How do I check out a RR if I want a more personal involvement and research?

P: You can look up a RR's history at the website of the Financial Industry Regulatory Authority (FINRA) and information can also be found at the SEC's website.

S: The same SEC we were just talking about? Can I trust it?

P: It is just part of the due diligence process.

A certified financial planner (CFP) can give you additional expertise with respect to taxes, insurance, employee benefits, and many other areas such as the ones we have covered. There are independent CFPs and many are part of groups.

S: Due diligence is needed here also.

P: Due diligence for all of the areas for sure. Two potential sources here are the Financial Planning Association and the National Association of Financial Planners.

S: What other acronyms do you have for me?

P: A registered investment advisor (RIA) will actually manage your money as they generally, not always, have the ability to make discretionary trades in your account.

S: What is a discretionary trade?

P: If you give someone the ability to make discretionary trades, they have the ability to make individual investments on your behalf without your consent each time. Proceed with caution here.

S: There must be more acronyms.

P: For sure, I'll give you two more. Chartered financial consultants (ChFC) are similar to CFPs but usually have more training in insurance and estate planning. Then, last but not least, are certified public accountants (CPAs) who offer financial planning services.

S: Accountants offering financial planning services?

P: You are forgetting one of our earliest discussions when I told you accountants are involved in aspects of business and operations that most people don't realize.

S: Well, I'll take the basic accounting class as you suggested, but nothing beyond that.

P: Your call.

S: Any way of checking the background of an advisor?

P: Yes, ask for Part 2 of Form ADV which requires investment advisers to provide prospective clients with a brochure and brochure supplements written in plain English. Among other information, it will tell you the background of the investment advisor firm and the firm's employees who provide advice.

S: Now what about the questions where you said you were deferring to someone else?

P: Yes, I enjoyed a column in the *Wall Street Journal* by Mr. Jason Zweig who had 19 potential questions to ask a potential financial adviser. (Zweig, 2017 August)

S: He expects you to ask 19 questions?

P: No, in a later article, he mentions only a couple may be relevant for you, but like everything else we have discussed, this is a good starting point. He even gives you the answer you should hear.

S: Okay, lay these questions on me.

P: The first one is, "Are you always a fiduciary, and will you state that in writing?" The answer should be yes.

S: Is the financial adviser a what?

P: A fiduciary has to act in your best interests. Many of the designations I have discussed are not bound by that standard so they could be selling you a product that, while suitable for you, may be generating them extra commissions than another product. There will always be conflicts, but hopefully far fewer with a fiduciary relationship. The other questions are as follows:

1. Does anybody else ever pay you to advise me and, if so, do you earn more to recommend certain products or services? (No)

2. Do you participate in any sales contests or awards programs creating incentives to favor particular vendors? (No)

3. Will you itemize all your fees and expenses in writing? (Yes)

4. Are your fees negotiable? (Yes)

5. Will you consider charging me by the hour or retainer instead of an annual fee based on my assets? (Yes)

S: I don't understand this one.

P: Some financial advisors will charge by the hour; some by a percentage of the assets. Say you are paying based on a percentage of assets. If you have $300,000 with them and are charged a 1.5 percent fee, you will be charged $4,500 no matter what happens during the year.

S: What if I don't meet with them during the year and my investments are losing money?

P: You will still be paying the 1.5 percent fee. Refunds in this industry are few and far between.

6. Can you tell me about your conflicts of interest, orally and in writing? (Yes, and no adviser should deny having any conflicts.)

7. Do you earn fees as an adviser to a private fund or other investments that you may recommend to me? (No)

8. Do you pay referral fees to generate new clients? (No)

9. Do you focus solely on investment management, or do you also advise on taxes, estates and retirement, budgeting and debt management, and insurance? (Here, the best answer depends on your needs as a client.)

10. Do you earn fees for referring clients to specialists like estate attorneys or insurance agents? (No)

11. What is your investment philosophy?

I'll interject here that it is critical that your risk/reward parameters be clearly defined to any prospective adviser. They should be asking you many questions to make sure they and you will be in sync here.

S: Risk versus reward, I knew you'd slip that in again.

P: Just like a curling four-foot putt.

12. Do you believe in technical analysis or market timing? (No)

13. Do you believe you can beat the market? (No)

14. How often do you trade? (As seldom as possible, ideally once or twice a year at most.)

You might have a different answer here, but make sure you clearly know the parameters.

15. How do you report investment performance? (After all expenses, compared with an average of highly similar

assets that includes dividends or interest income, over the long and short term.)

This one is difficult as there is no APR or APY as we saw when discussing banks.

16. Which professional credentials do you have and what are their requirements? (Among the best are CFA, CPA, and CFP. Many other financial certifications are marketing tools masquerading as fancy diplomas on an adviser's wall).

I may be exaggerating, but I once came across a guy who had about 10 sets of initials after his name who, I am now convinced, knows less than you at this point.

17. After inflation, taxes and fees, what is a reasonable estimated return on my portfolio over the long term? (If I told you anything over 3 percent to 4 percent annually, I'd be either naïve or deceptive.)

18. Who manages your money? (I do and I invest in the same assets I recommend to my clients.)

My former student Joe had a nice observation here. If it is a young individual or couple talking to an older financial adviser, they should certainly have different investment mixes.

S: Pretty comprehensive list.

P: Yes, it is, but I liked it. As I mentioned, you don't need to ask them all, but figure out the ones that are important to you.

Also, if you are married, your potential advisor should definitely want your spouse at meetings to make sure everyone is in sync.

S: Any advice here?

P: I'll defer to Mr. Zweig's expertise again. Meet with at least three potential advisers, ask them common questions, and shortly after each meeting, grade them on their responses. (Zweig, 2017 September) If married, do it as a couple.

S: I like this Mr. Zweig guy, but I have to ask a dumb question. Is it financial advisor or financial adviser?

P: I have always found his columns interesting and I will answer your question in a minute. I think we have reached the end so I will go back to my simplistic advice with respect to potential investments. These are clichés I have heard, but I have always relied on them.

S: Let's hear them.

P: Just two, firstly, if it sounds too good to be true, it probably is. Secondly, if you can't understand it in 10 minutes or less, you have no business investing in it. This would have served Bernie Madoff's clients well.

S: Why is that?

P: He never explained any investing technique to them. It was a "black box" formula which was too difficult to understand. Between this and constant 12 percent returns through good times and bad, red flags should have been going up.

Now with respect to advisor versus adviser, both are used with adviser being used more often by registered investment firms.

S: Well thanks Prof, this has certainly been a lengthy and interesting discussion.

P: Well I'll just look forward to you doing well so, sometime down the line, I'll have the pleasure of teaching you another lesson on the links while you are picking up the greens fees.

ACKNOWLEDGMENTS

I owe a debt of gratitude to many people who were kind enough to review different topics covered within and tell me where I misunderstood things or could have explained things better. Specifically, in no particular order, thank you to John Olson, Mike Fertitta, Bill Brewster, Rick Wallis, Paul Alix, Elizabeth Kueffel, Tricia Bruton, Erica Raiche, Eric Hett, Nate Fredette, and last, but certainly not least, Joe Latona. I'll single out Joe as he was a student in the course the first time I taught it in 2004 and has gone on (as a Theology major) to build a very successful Financial Planning practice. It was a pleasure picking his brain on different topics. Joe is quite representative of Saint Anselm graduates. With the core course structure at the school, students read, write, and discuss a wide variety of topics and develop a foundation for future success.

Thanks to Abby Mergenmeier, who did a great job of editing this book for me; Nina Cordes Spahn; and Gwen Verkuilen-Chevalier, Head of Collection Development and User Services, at the Geisel Library at Saint A's. Gwen wrote the references, which I would still be struggling to write, if she had not helped. Any mistakes in spelling, punctuation, or missed citations are solely my responsibility. Thanks also to retired Prof. John Romps who taught at Saint A's for 40+ years. I had the pleasure of having John in class and working with him as a colleague and he has always provided sound advice to me. Three Saint A's students, Kristen Brown, Clare Robbins, and Erica Hudson were quite helpful in the selection of the cover design of the book.

Lastly, I need to thank my wife Mary, who exhibited the usual patience with me, during this process, that she has exhibited while putting up with me for almost 36 years.

REFERENCES

Anand, K. (2016, November 2). Power of Compounding is the Eighth Wonder of the World; Here's How. *ETMarkets. com*. Retrieved from https://economictimes.indiatimes. com/markets/stocks/news/power-of-compounding-is-the-eighth-wonder-of-the-world-heres-how/article-show/55200424.cms

Andrews, M. (2017, October 11). Why A Long-Term Disability Policy is More Important than Pet Insurance. *National Public Radio*. Retrieved from https://www.npr.org/sections/health-shots/2017/10/11/556946744/why-a-long-term-disability-policy-is-more-important-than-pet-insurance

Barnett, J. and Berchick, E. (2017, September). Health Insurance Coverage in the United States: 2016. *Current Population Report: United States Census Bureau*. Retrieved from https://www.census.gov/library/publications/2017/demo/p60-260.html

Car Insurance in Massachusetts. (n.d.) Retrieved from https://www.dmv.org/ma-massachusetts/car-insurance.php

Chances of Disability: Me, Disabled? [Graphic illustration]. (n.d.). Retrieved from http://www.disabilitycanhappen. org/chances_disability/

Copeland, R. (2017, March 31). If You Have 29 Credit Cards, You're Probably a Millennial. *Wall Street Journal.* Retrieved from https://www.wsj.com/articles/if-you-have-29-credit-cards-youre-probably-a-millennial-1490972634

Damodaran, A. (2018, January 5). Annual Returns on Stock, T. Bonds and T Bills: 1928-Current [Data file]. Retrieved from http://pages.stern.nyu.edu/~adamodar/New_Home_Page/datafile/histretSP.html

Discover it Chrome Card for College Students. (n.d.). Retrieved from https://www.discover.com/credit-cards/student/chrome-card.html

Fay, B. What is a Stafford Loan? (n.d.). Retrieved from https://www.debt.org/students/types-of-loans/stafford/

Federal Reserve Bank of St. Louis, Economic Research. *1-Year Treasury Constant Maturity Rate (DGS1)* [Data file]. Retrieved from FRED, Federal Reserve Bank of St. Louis; https://fred.stlouisfed.org/series/DGS1, November 8, 2017.

Glader, P. (2008, December 16). Ahead of the Tape. *Wall Street Journal*, C1.

Glader, P. and Laise, E. (2009, February 28). GE Joins Parade of Deep Dividend Cuts. *Wall Street Journal*, A1.

Gryta, T. (2017, July 20). Business News: Old Money Problems Await New GE Boss. *Wall Street Journal,* B6.

Gryta, T. (2017, November 14). GE Takes Knife to Dividend. *Wall Street Journal,* A1.

How Much Should You Spend on Rent When Budgeting?. (n.d.). Retrieved from https://www.quicken.com/how-much-should-you-spend-rent-when-budgeting

If You Had Invested Right After Amazon's IPO. (2017, November 15). Retrieved from https://www.investopedia.com/articles/investing/082715/if-you-had-invested-right-after-amazons-ipo.asp

King, R. (2017, February 22). Study: Fewer Employers Offering Health Insurance. *Washington Examiner.* Retreived from http://www.washingtonexaminer.com/study-fewer-employers-offering-health-insurance/article/2615450

Loan Savings Calculator. (n.d.). Retrieved from https://www.myfico.com/credit-education/calculators/loan-savings-calculator/

A Look at the Shocking Student Loan Debt Statistics for 2018. (n.d.). Retrieved from https://studentloanhero.com/student-loan-debt-statistics/

Martin, C. Re: How to Cash In on Cash-Back Credit Cards. [Web log comment]. (2017, August 4). Retrieved from https://www.consumerreports.org/rewards-cards/how-to-cash-in-on-cash-back-credit-cards/

Mortgage Rates for Feb 16. (2018, February 16). Retrieved from https://www.bankrate.com/mortgage.aspx

Mutual Funds – Statistics and Facts [Graphic illustration]. (n.d.). Retrieved from https://www.statista.com/topics/1441/mutual-funds/

New Hampshire Department of Safety, Division of Motor Vehicles. (2018). *Financial Responsibility: Insurance Requirements/SR-22*. Retrieved from https://www.nh.gov/safety/divisions/dmv/financial-responsibility/insurance.htm

Rapoport, M. (2017, December 29). Who's the Center of Attention At Holiday Parties? The Tax Accountant. *Wall Street Journal*, B1.

Thomas, J. (2017, November 17). Where Have All the Public Companies Gone? *Wall Street Journal*. Retrieved from https://www.wsj.com/articles/where-have-all-the-public-companies-gone-1510869125

Total Net Assets of Mutual Funds in the United States from 1998 to 2016 (in trillion U.S. dollars). (n.d.). Retrieved from https://www.statista.com/statistics/255518/mutual-fund-assets-held-by-investment-companies-in-the-united-states/

Understanding Health Insurance Categories. (n.d.). Retrieved from https://www.healthcare.gov/choose-a-plan/plans-categories/

U.S. Department of Education, Federal Student Aid. *Subsidized and Unsubsidized Loans.* (n.d.). Retrieved from https://studentaid.ed.gov/sa/types/loans/subsidized-unsubsidized

Weidner, D. (2010, March 11). Harry Markopolos, SEC Chairman? *Wall Street Journal.* Retrieved from https://www.wsj.com/articles/SB1000142405274870435340457511 4482378869728

What's in Your Credit Score. (n.d.). Retrieved from https://www.myfico.com/credit-education/whats-in-your-credit-score/

Why Employers Check Credit and What They See. (2017, November 2). Retrieved from https://www.nerdwallet.com/blog/finance/credit-score-employer-checking/

Wilson, R. (2016, October 21). Obamacare News: Platinum Healthcare Exchange Plan Details. Retrieved from http://www.medicoverage.com/health-insurance-blog/news/platinum-healthcare-exchange-plan

Woolley, S. (2006, November 13). Inside America's Richest Insurance Racket. *Forbes.com.* Retrieved from https://www.forbes.com/free_forbes/2006/1113/148_2.html

Zweig, J. (2017, August 26). The Intelligent Investor: A Grand Inquisition in 19 Easy Questions. *Wall Street Journal,* B1.

Zweig, J. (2017, September 9). The Intelligent Investor: In Sum, Grill an Advisor and Always Keep Score. *The Wall Street Journal,* B1.